The author when he worked for his living, 1947
Photograph by John Taylor

BEVIN BOY –
A RELUCTANT MINER

BEVIN BOY –
A RELUCTANT MINER

Reg Taylor

ATHENA PRESS
LONDON

BEVIN BOY – A RELUCTANT MINER
Copyright © Reg Taylor 2004

ISBN 1 84401 345 6

First Published 2004 by
ATHENA PRESS
Queen's House, 2 Holly Road
Twickenham, TW1 4EG
United Kingdom

Printed for Athena Press

To the two Peters and all the miners I worked with.

A trammer in a crossgate working with an oil safety lamp.
Author's sketch

Foreword

It is largely due to one man that I now sit here writing these simple notes, memories and recollections that have lodged at the back of my mind for nearly sixty years.

During the later years of the Second World War, 1939-1945, there was a looming fuel crisis. The indiscriminate conscription of working coal miners had brought about a shortage of much-needed coal production.

Ernest Bevin, born in 1881 in Somerset, became one of the most powerful union leaders in the first half of the twentieth century. During the war he emerged as a force to be reckoned with as Minister of Labour and National Service in Churchill's Coalition Government. In this role it fell to him to find a solution to the growing coal crisis. At first it seemed easy. Miners would not be called up for National Service and others could volunteer for work in the mining industry, instead of serving in the armed forces.

This scheme did not yield a supply of miners sufficient to end the crisis. The next step was to recruit every tenth conscript who registered for national service and direct him for work in the mining industry. Even this was inadequate and so it became necessary to recruit every fifth man to register and send to the mines.

The unfortunate conscripts were to be known as 'Bevin Boys' after the originator of the scheme. It did not gain universal approbation. Many thought of it as a form of industrial slavery. Indeed the change of life-style would be a culture shock – as they say nowadays – to many who found themselves embarking on a vastly different career structure, myself included.

But no matter how soul-destroying they were to find their new existence, it was of little consolation to be reminded of the thousands and thousands of former miners who, before them, had been condemned to a life of subterranean toil over the centuries, miners driven there quite simply by the economic whip of necessity, where son followed father, and so on.

Ernest Bevin, most certainly, was the cause of my abrupt and lasting change of career. It is largely due to the relentless pressure of friends and former colleagues whose insistence I can no longer resist, that I sit down to put on record what they think must be a host of fascinating episodes. For myself, I have never thought of them as being relatively interesting. Anyone with sufficient patience will doubtless form their own opinions. Now read on…

The author at the 2002 Durham Miners' Gala
Photograph by P Thompson

To a Brave New World

There was I, approaching my eighteenth birthday, aware that soon I would register for national service. I was living away from home, working as a junior civilian employee in the county constabulary. I was at the very bottom of the ladder and while lucky to be in this position, it had never occurred to me the remote possibility that someday I might make chief constable. If every soldier has a Field Marshall's baton in his knapsack, there was no reason why I should not have a chief constable's swagger cane in mine. As it happens, I didn't. But this was sheer fantasy. I had been brought up in a social stratum where it was sufficient of an achievement to be in employment, never mind to have the ambitious dreams of sheer fantasy which were only for rich people.

However, the war was something far away and only touched me in the many inconveniences and shortages that all civilians suffered. As a police employee, I did have one mark of distinction which raised me a small degree above the common throng. This was my gas mask. Where civilians had the relatively flimsy rubber self-contained mask, and the Civil Defence personnel also had self-contained masks a little more robust but with a ridiculous outlet-control valve which could be made to produce rude noises, I had a proper War Department mask. That was one where a flexible tube connected the facepiece to the filter unit carried in a canvas sort of bag. I looked like somebody important to the war effort. Such was the state of my naïve innocence.

I had two colleagues slightly older than myself in the same department who were keen to join the Royal Air Force. They were keen to volunteer as the unpopular Bevin Boy scheme had already started and they hoped to avoid being drafted to the mines by enlisting in the forces. As it happens this would have made no difference; if their numbers came up they would have been chosen for mine work. My colleagues went into the Royal Air Force. Eventually they were replaced by another junior civilian employee and I became the senior of the two of us. My pay was raised to £1 per week, but I did get my keep.

Many of the policemen were ex-miners who had found a better life in the police force and were glad of the change. I was often very much the butt of their jokes as so often junior civilian employees were, but I got an insight into their ways and consequently got to know a little of the miner's way of life and I suspect I was not really a very unpopular 'civvie'.

I registered for national service and was sent to that fascinating town, Huddersfield, for my medical. I was examined, hit with rubber hammers, made to cough, and my eyesight and hearing were tested. Much to my surprise I was told that I had passed my medical 'A1'. They gave me a shilling; I believe this was the King's Shilling. I now wish that I had kept it. I cannot remember how I spent it.

I returned to work and found that I was due a week's holiday. I took advantage of this week to extend my knowledge of the Yorkshire Dales, which even with the restricted transport of wartime, were within relatively easy reach. Just a couple of bus rides and then a bit of healthy leg stretching would soon get me out in the heart of God's own county. I could stay cheaply if not always in the greatest luxury at the many well-placed youth hostels in the area.

I had seen enticing pictures of Mastiles Lane, the green lane which climbed over the limestone hills between Malhamdale and the glories of Wharfedale. I could not rest until I had trodden this exhilarating route for myself. And so I set off on my lonely trek armed with a pre-war Ordnance Survey Map of the terrain I wished to cover. I had seen a few enthusiastic books on the area and was an eager reader of the embrionic *Yorkshire Dalesman*, as it was first known. But few of these warned that the sun did not always shine on the Yorkshire Dales.

The rain was relentless. Rain, rain, rain! It drove in from the west over the moor tops. There was scarcely any shelter just the limestone walls which bounded Mastiles Lane, one of the glorious green lanes of the Western Yorkshire Dales which in better weather was truly a path to Paradise.

I had caught an early bus to Malham from Skipton.

Undeterred by the weather, I got off this bus at my destination in a gathering shower. With all the brash confidence of a headstrong seventeen-year old, I was determined to set off whatever the weather. After all, the bus fare was a lot for a young fellow with his foot only just on the threshold of life. Having got so far it was unthinkable to turn back.

This was late in 1944. The traverse of Mastiles Lane from Malham to Threshfield and Linton in the Craven Dales of West Yorkshire was an ambition of long standing. I looked at the swollen waterfalls of Gordale Scar, and suitably impressed, set off determined to achieve my objective.

Steadily I trudged up the lane through the driving rain, my War Department surplus anti-gas cape not totally adequate for the conditions but better than the more usual cycle capes used by walkers of the day.

The rain was oozing through the lace holes of my strong shoes. I could not afford walking boots then. I snuggled up for a while in the lee of the wall, shoving a few sheep out of the way. But it was not very comfortable. I decided to press on and eventually I found myself overlooking the Wharfe valley much sooner than I had expected. I was soaked to the skin, in a way that does not seem to happen to walkers nowadays.

After a long damp slog, the green lane became a narrow tarmac road which eventually joined one of the major thoroughfares of Wharfedale. In the torrential downpour I was beginning to feel that the call of the open road was not all that I had been led to believe, and that the wind on the heath could be overdone, when – lo and behold – a bus, rare in wartime days turned up unexpectedly. I soon realised that this would take me to Ilkley. With a flash of inspiration I abandoned my plans for a walking tour in the dales and jumped on the bus. I might be wet, but this vehicle would carry me part of the way home.

Shivering and damp I walked up our garden path to the surprise of my parents. My father greeted me with a welcome not devoid of irony as I walked into the house. 'Bit damp for walking, lad?' I sheepishly acknowledged his welcome – then, 'There's a letter for thee.' It was in an official buff-looking envelope. My heart leapt. My call up papers! Soon I would be at the controls of one of those graceful little Tiger Moths that used to buzz about the summer skies training future pilots in the initial stages of aerial warfare.

I opened the letter. It reminded me that I had passed my medical 'A1', and there was the information that I had been selected for service in the coal mining industry. This was couched in such terms that suggested this was a great honour.

In the Beginning...

It was in the early hours of the day after Boxing Day – 5.30 a.m. to be precise. It was pitch black, apart from a few twinkling stars peeping between the high-sided wool warehouses. Pitch black, of course, because it was wartime and in the blackout. It was bitterly cold and the frost was beginning to bite, ice was forming on the stone pavement, but I noticed nothing of this. With my head down in my scarf, I was concerned about catching the 6 a.m. train to Leeds, the first part of the journey to my new destiny. I would have to change there for Tibshelf, near Pontefract. Despite the cold I was in a bit of a sweat. I was nearing the end of my three-mile walk to the station. Deep in thought about what was in store for me, I plodded on, my father's words echoing in my mind.

'Now then, lad, don't look on the black side.' – this was not meant as a pun. 'You Bevin Boys have been chosen by a democratic process' – a simple form of lottery. 'As I was saying, lad, you've been chosen by a democratic process. You now have one foot safely on the first step of the social ladder.

'With one in five of the choice of the nation's young men selected for the pits you are sure to find yourself rubbing shoulders with young sons of the aristocracy, the nobs and the nobility. Play your cards right, lad and you could soon be on visiting terms with the county set, invited to the mansions of the fine people. I never had a chance like this.'

Now I was on the first stage of my journey to the training colliery at Pontefract, about twenty-five miles away. I had been given a railway warrant which would enable me to get there. It meant catching a train from one of the town's two stations at 6 a.m. This was in the middle of winter. That is why I was making the three-mile walk into town carrying my tatty suitcase at this ungodly hour. As it frequently happens it does not really begin to freeze until the last hours before daybreak. This was no exception.

The stars suddenly wheeled in their courses, I lost my orientation, and landed with a thump on my backside. I had slipped on the icy cobbles of the road's surface. Lost in my dreams I had not paid enough attention to where I was putting my feet. I sat there in the middle of the road, relatively safe for there was no traffic in those days. This was an inauspicious start to my career as a miner. By good fortune I had fallen on to the small suitcase which contained my few possessions. It could have been a lot worse. Or it could have been a lot better; I might have broken my back and would have escaped my new career and not be sat there absorbed in idle reminiscence about a black future.

Well, this would be something to chat about to my new colleagues. The station was virtually deserted apart from a weary looking train with small groups of zombie-like figures standing nearby. They all had the characteristic attitudes of those condemned to be up and about in the hours that are still the middle of the night. Nobody was cheerful. But eventually they all agreed that we were bound for a new life in an unknown industry. We would stick together; there might be safety in numbers.

One member of our miserable band looked, and was, more wretched than the rest of us. It turned out that in a fit of unrestrained patriotism he had volunteered to be a miner and was regretting it already. He had not improved the situation by having overindulged the night before and was suffering the consequences. We kept our distance; his rumbling stomach was far from reassuring.

I tried to break the ice, even though it had already nearly broken me. I would initiate a conversation.

We were all bound for the Prince of Wales Colliery at Pontefract – the 'Pontyprince' as it was known. Tibshelf station was the nearest station and the place where we would all get off the train. We were in a compartment of a suburban stopping train with no corridor. I asked if anybody knew Tibshelf and remarked on what an unusual name this was. My new colleagues were unanimous in their reply, 'It's a bloody stupid name.'

That was all I managed to get out of them until we neared the station where we could see the lattice-girdered skeleton of the tall pit-head gear rising out of the dawn mist of the winter morning. We began the trudge of about three-quarters of a mile to this gaunt symbol which was to be the landmark of our prospective industrial slavery.

That Sinking Feeling

I have already mentioned that it was approximately a three-quarters mile walk from the station to the colliery where we were to learn our new trade as miners. We all had a sense of foreboding, we timid apprehensive recruits, making our way along the pit lane through the fields, which in sunnier times would yield golden crops from the soil above the hundreds of feet of strata sitting on the coal-seam.

But we had no thoughts of golden crops waving in the summer sunshine as the tall dark tower with its endlessly spinning wheels beckoned us on to a life where colour would be non-existent. Now the reality of our new lives began to sink in, as a grim foreboding began to dispel the former artificial cheeriness we had sustained on our journey here.

How on earth did I find myself in this situation? What had gone wrong? The empty feeling in the pit of my stomach did nothing to ease the feeling of rejection by society, or to convince me that there could be any truth in the encouraging remarks of old friends and well-wishers. Already they belonged to a world in the rapidly receding past.

I was not well-versed in politics and like my new colleagues found difficulty in believing that Mr Ernest Bevin could be a good politician.

The war had gone on for four years now and an ever increasing need for coal had to be satisfied. The nation needed more coal than its mining force could produce. Here was a demonstration of the government's amazing capability for forward thinking. Someone in power should have known that miners should have been placed on the reserved occupation list. Doubtless they had other things on their collective mind.

So it was decided to recruit conscripts for service in the mining industry. At first it was every tenth person to register for national service who was so directed. This was then found to be insufficient; after that it became every fifth person to register. There was no appeal; it was either the mines or prison.

'Nye' Bevan, another politician with a similar sounding name to Ernest, was later to say that this country could survive forever because its very foundations were built on coal. Why did no one recognise this at the outbreak of hostilities?

Thus it was that I now stood under the shadow of the Pontyprince's pit-head gear, wondering what it was going to be like down there. The thought of where my next meal was to come from, and where I would lay my head that night were the least of my worries. Although these facilities were assured.

It wasn't as bad as all that. We reported and were registered to make sure we had all turned up. We were greeted by instructors, former miners, who were on the whole cheerful and helpful. They seemed to appreciate our perplexity and did their best to inspire us with confidence. Soon we were issued with shiny new helmets and rugged Toetector boots. We were told where the canteen was and that a bus would collect us to take us to the hostel that would be our home for a month. We were advised to make the most of this month of instruction – it would be the last holiday we would have for some time.

Now we were beginning to feel a little bit braver, although now, looking back at the photographs which were in the papers nearly sixty years ago, we looked like overconfident children. Our first few days were spent in classroom instruction. There were no exams at the end. There was no point. It did not matter whether we were brilliant students or untrainable misfits, at the end of the course we were going down the pits, like it or not. Part of our training was physical education. If the weather was clement we performed all sorts of physical feats on the grass of the nearby Pontefract racecourse. If the weather did not permit we did the same indoors – that is, in the tote sheds, where in happier days confident punters would place their bets.

It was not long before we were to go underground for the first time. Most recruits were unhappy about this but the instructor reminded us that we were not the first – nor would we be the last.

The instructor informed us that the shaft was only about 700 yards deep. The one we would go down would be the oldest in the complex; the rest of the mine was still engaged in essential coal production. Being the oldest, it still had wooden guide rails for the cages instead of the more usual tight guide ropes. This meant we might find that the ride may not be as comfortable as it would have been in more up-to-date surroundings.

Still we would probably pay half a crown for a similar thrill at Blackpool. Our instructor also tried to explain to us the phenomena of acceleration and deceleration. The shaft was 700 yards deep and it only took about three minutes or so to make the descent – an alarming speed to the novice. He warned us that as we neared the end of the descent we would all be convinced that the powers that were, had decided it was all a big mistake and they had decided to pull us back out again. 'Don't be taken in!' he warned.

The following morning we climbed the steps to the pit-head bank, where the kindly old banksman ushered us into the cage like rats into a trap. I am unable to remember how many of us it held – there were four different decks – but soon we were all locked safely in. We couldn't get out if we wanted. The banksman gave his fateful signal and the cage plummeted towards the centre of the earth. It took our breath away. We clung to whatever we could and stared helplessly at the sides of the shaft, the details of which were rendered indistinguishable by the speed we were falling. Then it began – at first the same sort of feeling experienced in the slow moving lifts of department stores when they began to go up. But it got stronger and stronger. We were all convinced we were on the way back to the surface. It was impossible to tell by looking at the sides of the shaft. The cage was slowing down as the winding engine man began to brake. We were not convinced that we were still going down, until the cage came to a final stop at the bottom of its run.

Still a bit scared and shaky we were helped out of the cage by the onsetter – the man who controlled the loading and unloading of the cage at the pit bottom. There we stood, a group of frightened conscripted miners contemplating for the first time the gloom and characteristic smell of a deep pit, the unforgettable odour of air which has circulated for miles underground, and owes some of its pungent quality to the pony stables. A new life was opening to us.

How to be a Miner

The descent was quite alarming in its way, but had not been as terrifying as we thought it might have been. We were in an old shaft and the cages ran in well-worn wooden guides, not the more usual taut cable guides which gave a much smoother ride. This was wartime and we were taking part in a desperate measure to help to save the country in which the comfort of embryo Bevin Boys was not of much great importance. At the pit bottom we were helped out of the cage by the onsetter, the man whose duty it was to load the full tubs into the cage at the pit bottom and to get the empty ones out. In this case he was a distinguished-looking man everybody called Ambrose. His tall slender figure and fine aquiline profile – he reminded us of Basil Rathbone – gave the distinct feeling that he was not in his natural environment. But here was one of the first lessons – that you can't judge by appearances. Apparently he was of stalwart mining stock and a respected member of the team entrusted with our training. If you could have people like that working underground there was a glimmer of hope for us unwilling recruits.

We stood around in timid groups sniffing the air and wondering what would happen next. We were at the bottom of the upcast shaft, that is, one that was used to extract the air from, and thus ventilate the entire mine. At the top was a powerful centrifugal fan. This pulled the air from the pit, after it had circulated through every underground nook and cranny – including the stables. These added that unforgettable, distinctive touch of piquancy. I can still call it to mind today, sixty years afterwards.

Our reactions were divided. The brave extroverts who had bragged that there was nothing to the first descent were now distinctly quiet while those of us who were cowards at heart were feeling more confident. It was an adventure and had not been as bad as we expected. We were now broken up into groups and led off by underground instructors. Their purpose was to explain and demonstrate the basic systems of underground coal transport, but this did not include conveyors. Our instructor began by describing to us, as he led us off away from the pit bottom, the theory and practice of the 'endless rope-haulage systems'. I would have been much happier had he told us something about the theory and practice of holding the roof up. There was now a vertical distance of 700 yards between me and God's daylight and the sweet icy December air. The relatively brightly lit area at the pit bottom was receding quickly as we stumbled along the haulage way increasing my doubts about the ability of this 700 yards of rock strata to stay in position above me.

Soon we came to a rope-hauled tramway. As the instructor began his spiel I gradually began to forget about the 700 yards of rock just waiting to flatten me to pulp. The endless rope was there before me slowly snaking through the Stygian gloom, the monotony of its unceasing journey relieved by various pulleys smoothing the way between the tracks, through the all-pervading dust, and round barrel-shaped pulleys on vertical axles where there was a corner.

'*You must never get on the wrong side of the rope at corners!*' This was the stern warning our instructor gave to us. With an innate sense of drama, he then demonstrated his lyrical descriptive powers as he enthusiastically recounted the horrible disasters that had befallen those who had chosen to ignore this simple rule. I imagine he would have been good at describing the lives – and spectacular deaths – of some of the more obscure saints.

The rope went round passageways and headings set up for demonstration and training purposes. The tubs, or mine cars as the Americans like to call them, each held ten hundredweight of coal when full. This was in the days before metrication, so in fact it would be approximately half (0.5) of a metric tonne. Fortunately they were all empty. They came along grumbling and squeaking out of the dark, lashed to the haulage rope with lengths of chain with heavy iron hooks at each end.

We were to learn the technique of lashing on and unlashing. The instructor showed us how. It was easy. Nothing to it. All that was needed was some agility and a bit of confidence, and preferably a pair of tough leather gloves. But these we had not got. It was here that I began to appreciate the theatrical complaint about the 'innate animosity of inanimate objects'.

After watching the instructor pick up the chain, hook one end on to the front of the tub, flick the other end over the rope, then wrap it round twice and hook it back on to itself as the rope trundled along, I volunteered to be the first to have a go. This was before I had learnt the folly of volunteering for anything.

I tried to pick up one end of the chain. It did not want to leave the ground. I had never trained as a weight lifter. I managed to get it up to shoulder height, desperately trying not to trip up over the rails as the three empty tubs challenged me with their own form of dumb insolence. With one mighty effort I managed to hurl the hook over the rope and eventually hooked it on to itself to an accompaniment of guffaws from my fellow trainees.

The chain gripped the rope and the three tubs went grumbling on their way. It came as a shock when the instructor told me to run after the tubs and lash the last tub to the rope. The run of three tubs had to be secured at each end. We couldn't do with them running away could we?

After my clumsy effort I felt like slinking off into the darkness to nurse my battered pride. I did not want to be a miner, and nothing in this episode convinced me that I was cut out to be a capable miner. Having caused my colleagues some amusement at my attempts, I never thought of watching them. I was taking a swig from my bottle of cold tea when I heard a torrent of invective.

I looked up and to my satisfaction could see the instructor using the emergency stop to extricate a colleague from a situation featuring runaway tubs, a disaster I had narrowly avoided. No one laughed now.

This was an early important lesson – if you don't do it properly you get hurt. Next, having learnt how to get the tubs in motion on the endless rope, we had to learn how to stop free-running tubs gravitating down an incline. This technique was known as 'lockering'. Simply it was a matter of shoving something like an old pick handle between the spokes of the cast iron wheels, thus locking an axle and creating a braking effect. We walked along the heading to a point at which there was a down gradient.

The tubs were unlashed from the rope and gravity did the rest. The tubs were to be arrested near the bottom of the slope before they gained too much speed. Here there sat another tutor, Alf, an obvious expert in the art of lockering. At his side was a triangular pile of old pick handles arranged at right angles to the track. We were told to watch carefully as a run of three tubs came trundling down the slope gradually gathering speed.

We noticed in Alf's eyes the steely glint of the hunter on the verge of securing his prey, even in the dark, dusty, suffocating atmosphere which filled our lungs with evil blackness.

Alf sat still and motionless, then like the release of tightly coiled steel spring, Alf was galvanised into action. Without getting up from his sitting position using one arm only, he flung six of these handles with the precision of a darts champion into the spaces between the spokes of the six wheels.

The run of tubs came to a sudden halt. It was a spectacular demonstration. Looking at me, he said, 'Nah then lad, you do it!' Nonchalantly he walked a few yards (metres, I should really be saying) down the slope and we waited for the next three tubs to arrive. I had taken his position at the side of the pile of lockers. We did not have long to wait, and I was now accustomed to making a fool of myself, so what the heck. I managed to get two of the six lockers into the wheels slowing the tubs down but not stopping them. Alf, with all the skill of an expert, quickly and easily stopped the tubs before they ran away out of control.

I looked at Alf and he came out with, 'Not bad, lad. Ah'll shew thee haa to do it properly naa.' He retrieved the lockers and waited for the next set of tubs to come trundling down.

He walked at the side of them slipping a locker into each wheel; the run came to a steady halt. 'Try agen,' he said. I did. It was easy. From then on I always stayed at the back of the crowd.

I was now beginning to forget my fear of the 700 yards of rock strata between me and daylight, and getting used to the all-penetrating dust and the unquenchable thirst which it inevitably raised. And so we recruits began to slip in to the training routine which, in my case, was to bear little relationship to what I would have to do when I became a full-time miner.

Life Goes On

And so the days passed by. Mornings were spent in practical underground training, the afternoons in lectures and physical training – whether we needed it or not. I had always inclined towards the teaching of St Paul, particularly in one of his letters to St Timothy: 'Bodily exercise profiteth little' (I:Timothy:IV;8). But this was to no avail. If the weather was appropriate we would run round the nearby race-track; if not, we made use of the betting offices which were empty inside and provided a crude improvised gymnasium.

There we would do what they used to call 'physical jerks' until we began to sweat, or as a diversion we would have a tug of war. I found that I could surreptitiously tie the end of my team's rope round one of the upright girders that was a main roof support. This did not help us to win, but at least we did not lose. Some members of my intake complained that we had to get changed in what was a public loo, but they were given the alternative of changing into their gym kit outside, which was a bit rough in December.

At the end of the day we were collected by a number of motor coaches which took us to our hostel. This was at Cutsyke, a suburb of Castleford. Anybody who thought that Jarrow was a depressing place should have tried looking at Castleford as it was then. The eternal dust found its way out of the local collieries and settled on window ledges, fences or any reasonably level surface. Apart from its rugby (league), Castleford did not have much to encourage the visitor.

The hostel itself, was something like a collection of Nissen huts, but at least more cheerfully decorated than you would find in the army. There were dormitories, a canteen, and a common room – a sort of concert/assembly room with piano.

I don't remember much about the food; it was wholesome and I remember no complaints. The tea was, of course, excellent. Pit canteen tea is the best in the world and you would always want to drink gallons of it after finishing a shift.

Sitting round the coal fires is a long-remembered joy. There were semicircles of easy chairs, arranged round the fireplaces. These were soon filled after the evening meal. Many would rush their meal in order to get one on the front row, near to the fire. But most of us were completely tired out and did not want to do much more than sit and read, or just sit and gaze at the cheery fire, the value of whose fuel we were now beginning to appreciate.

Those who sat nearest the fire were warmer than those on the outside, the latecomers. And so the nightly game of musical chairs would begin. Those who occupied the chairs nearest the fire were those who got there first, and consequently, were the first who would need to answer the call of nature. As soon as someone got up out of his hard-won fireside chair it would be seized by a chillier mortal from the row behind. A bit like the patrons of the celebrated *Windmill Theatre* who would begin at the back of the auditorium and make their way to the coveted front row, but for different reasons. And then it would be his turn to want to go for a pee. Some could manage to get to the front row twice in a night but usually just in time for lights out.

The administrative staff tried to make us comfortable and would organise entertainments other than the inevitable ping-pong, board games and beetle drives. Wednesday night was talent night. Anybody who thought he had some ability to entertain in any reasonable way, was encouraged to do so on a stage at one end of the large common room.

There was a public address system and a member of staff, a more mature lady, who was an accomplished pianist with a large repertoire, and who could play in a range of different styles and would readily adapt to the performer she accompanied. Those who had the temerity to volunteer to exhibit their performing powers had to join a queue and explain to the 'producer' and the pianist what they intended to do. There was no audition or any form of weeding out process, the result being a diverse array of talent as entertaining as it was unexpected.

In one of those moments of rashness, which have dogged me all my life – I have never learnt from my experiences – I joined the queue of volunteers. I had some success at family and friendly parties of reciting what in those days were considered to be humorous monologues. I admired Billy Bennett – who never made it into the gentry – but could never capture his inimitable style. I told the organisers I would give them *The Cremation of Sam Magee*. Yes this would do – did I want any musical accompaniment? The lady pianist suggested *In a Monastery Garden*, but I had to explain that this was not really appropriate.

I began to doubt the wisdom of my readiness to volunteer to entertain. Viewing the faces of my former friendly comrades in adversity from behind the footlights, I now recognised them to be a vicious horde of hooligans baying for the blood of anyone who dared to face them from the stage. The performer – a would-be crooner – who ventured on the stage before me appeared to have everything under control.

He sauntered on in one of those beltless tweedy overcoats, popular in those days, a trilby hat nonchalantly perched on the back of his head and puffing at a pipe which he casually removed from his mouth as he approached the microphone.

The pianist began, very convincingly, with the opening bars and theme of *When the Blue of the Night*...

It was at this moment that our singer took his eyes, firmly fixed on the microphone, away from that accessory and looked at the audience. There was a hushed moment of awful silence. He shoved his pipe into a pocket and said, with great conviction, 'Aw, bugger it!'

The audience waited in eager anticipation to see how the act was to continue. The silence continued, then, with a look of abject terror, he fled from the stage. The applause was thunderous, punctuated with cries of 'Encore! More! More, bring the bugger back,' and so on.

Now it was my turn...

How my heart sank as I faced this raucous audience. It sank even further when the pianist began the schmaltzy strains of *In a Monastery Garden*. I turned to her saying, 'No. No not that!' The music stopped. I turned again to the audience, ready to start again, wondering what sort of a mess this was I had got myself into. I took a deep breath and before I could get the first words out, the schmaltzy sounds of *Bells across the Meadow* drifted across the stage. I took my courage in both hands as they say, and began:

> There are strange things done,
> in the midnight Sun,
> By the men who moil for gold,
> The Northern Lights have seen strange sights
> But the strangest they ever did see...

I could go no further.

In loud stentorian tones, from the back of the hall came the question, 'What does moil mean?'

I had to reply, 'It's what we will all soon be doing, but moiling for coal, not gold!' My interrogator appeared to be satisfied with this answer and there were signs of approval from others. I tried to resume my dramatic narrative...

> But the strangest they ever did see,
> Was that night on the marge
> Of the Lake Labarge,
> That I cremated Sam Magee

I tried to rattle this out with each syllable like one of a string of bullets from a Gatling gun. But no, another voice wanted to know what I meant by the word 'Marge' and another wanted to know where the bloody hell the Lake Labarge was. Was I making all this up? And so it went on. I managed to get to the end, fielding off many and various interruptions, but yet establishing some friendly relationship with the audience. One of the last comments was that if Sam Magee thought it was cold on the Yukon trail, he should have tried living in our hostel. There was applause and somebody asked if I knew any more.

Inflamed with my success I started up again with *The Shooting of Dangerous Dan Magrew*. I hardly got to the end of the first line, when I was encouraged to leave the stage by two of the administrators who pointed out that somebody else wanted to have a go.

The next day passed without much excitement, but sitting in the pit canteen – as I have already said, pit canteens served the best tea in the whole world – I was idly musing over my sad fate when Charlie came and sat next to me. I had not met him before and he asked if he could sit at this adjacent vacant seat. There was no reason why I should object. He was a year or two older than me but a volunteer trainee. 'That was very brave and sporting of you last night. Do you do that sort of thing often?' My answer to this was 'no' and that last night's performance was certainly my last.

We talked about other things and then he told me that he had made friends with some miners at the *Star and Garter* in Castleford. Did I fancy going for a pint and meeting them? They liked to play dominoes; could I make up a fourth?

When I said I could play dominoes I told a white lie. I wasn't sure about the pint either. I was thinking of the simple game I had played many years previously with my dear old lonely grandmother. I had no real concept of the game, which even now I do not fully understand. How on earth do the experts know every card in every hand after the first two have been played? So with cheerful innocence, I ventured to the *Star and Garter* with Charlie. Though he was a much better player than I would ever be, he was still over-young to be a hardened expert.

We arrived at the pub in the dark, in the blackout, in Castleford – a grim combination. I don't know what that town is like now; little has happened to make me want to go back, but it must have improved.

I had read about Jarrow. In fact I saw the Jarrow Marchers arrive in London, albeit as a child of nine. I had been moved by JB Priestley's account of the town, but when I did eventually see Jarrow, admittedly twenty years or so after the march, I thought it was as a garden city compared to my impressions of Castleford. I will no doubt get it in the neck for that!

Charlie's friends were already in place, their backs to the window, pints in front of them with dominoes and board all set up ready for the fray. They were typical South Yorkshire miners: well-scrubbed bony faces, piercingly blue eyes, their eyelids finely lined with the ingrained trace of coal dust that no amount of soap could move. They looked as if they were extras for an early expressionist movie. Our welcome was cheerful. Did we want a game of dominoes? Of course. Best of five? – that was Charlie and I against them. Yes. Right we'll play for pints.

They did not mean that when a player had become the victor in a best of five contest, a round of drinks would be bought. Oh no, these were accomplished drinkers. They wanted the losers after each hand to pay for a round of pints. A rough calculation of the worst scenario was the possibility that thirty-six pints would be bought before an ultimate winner was declared. My heart sank – I was going to be the loser; how would I pay off my gambling debts? But even worse, how would I drink my victory libations if I won?

I remember but few details of the game, but that a situation had arisen where I, a complete novice, had upset the strategy of the experts.

They had little idea of what I was going to do next – I hadn't a clue myself. I cannot remember how many hands I won, still less how much beer I got down, but eventually we parted company. Our miner friends said they had thoroughly enjoyed the evening and hoped we would go again. I said I would if I could remember where it was. Charlie was not quite as far gone as I was. He steered me home to our hostel, where we were greeted with much amusement. My comrades had made an apple-pie bed of my folding-type camp bed, but not only that, they had balanced it on its retractable legs so that at the slightest touch it would collapse. As I tried to get into it, it did and the world began to shake as if overwhelmed by an earthquake. I suddenly remembered that tomorrow I was to learn how to drive pit ponies. Oh, Heaven, do not forsake me…!

A collier at work in a twenty-two-inch seam

Author's sketch

Transports of Delight

It is always a pleasure to see someone who enjoys his work, the man who fulfils his allotted task to the best of his ability, no matter how humble the duty or how limited his capacity. Such a person was the one who woke us up in our hostel each morning. I never found out what else he did but at 5 a.m. each morning his joy knew no bounds.

First of all, he would hammer at the door of our tiny Nissen hut dormitory. Then he would pick up a pair of mining boots and with all the skill of a nine-pin bowler he would hurl them down the aisle which separated the beds of the slumbering trainee miners. Just to make sure, he then bellowed, 'Come on my lucky lads – let's be having you up bright and early!' The unlucky sleeper who did not respond to this hearty invitation would find himself without his blankets, exposed to the bracing air of our chilly hut.

On this particular morning my reluctance to awaken was tempered by trepidation at thoughts of learning how to control a beast of burden – the pit pony. I was not happy in the presence of horses. A few years previously I had fallen off a horse on the sands at Morecambe. The only injury I suffered was to my pride, but even so the incident left me with an indelible mental scar. It was bad enough being in close proximity to a horse in the open air but what would it be like in the narrow confines of a haulage heading where the pony wanted to be even less than I did? I was not antagonistic to animals, but I preferred those which were smaller than me, such as dogs, cats, guinea pigs or hamsters.

On arrival at the pit 'bank' I and another trainee, Albert, whom I never saw again, were selected to ride in the deck of the cage which had a separate means of exit. We sat obediently on the floor where we had been told to by the supervisor and were surprised when the cage stopped some distance from the bottom of the shaft.

'Okay, this is where you get out!' Albert and I were thunderstruck. It was pitch dark. We were not at the bottom of the shaft. We could see nowhere to get out to. We looked at the instructor hoping this was some sort of joke, but no. He shone his high candle-power lamp and then we could see we were opposite an opening in the shaft wall. Indicating the opening which was some sort of roadway, he then told us to get out, sit there and wait. We waited for what seemed a lifetime, then a gnome-like figure appeared out of the darkness, exchanged a greeting with the instructor – who was still in the cage – then signalled to the surface that the cage could continue its downward plunge.

The gnome offered us no greeting. In the surrounding darkness he looked as if he had never been to the surface, that his entire existence was spent underground. It may have been that he was born down here or, more likely, was created by some primeval parthenogenetic process. 'Follow me,' he grunted. We had no alternative. The roadway we were in began to drift downwards. After an indeterminate time we saw lights in the distance, and the characteristic smell of pony stables got stronger. Deep pits have a smell all their own, the flavour of which is strengthened by the presence of ponies, a scent which I am grateful never to experience again.

As I followed the gnome down the drift to the stables I mused on the apparent cruelty of keeping and working ponies underground. It was bad enough for us who had some understanding of why we were there, but what was it like for the poor creatures who spent a lifetime underground, never seeing the light of day or breathing fresh air? I am still not convinced that it was not a universal legal cruelty.

Having said that, I soon discovered that the underground stables provided much better, cleaner conditions for their charges than many on the surface. The stablemen looked after their charges; they were regularly groomed and well cared for. There were stories of stablemen who gave up holidays to look after the ponies when the pit was having its annual break although I must say I never met any.

I never had any ambition to be an equestrian. When you are riding a horse you cannot see its face, and consequently have no idea what it is thinking. Take a dog for a walk and there is a constant dialogue of communication between you and your charge, but I could not see how this could happen with a horse.

I was introduced to the pony which was to be my charge for most of the shift. His name was Boxer, a name which struck fear into the heart of a peaceful sort of person like myself. I tried to make contact with the creature, but this was almost impossible since his forehead was protected by a thick leather guard and his eyes were almost hidden by strong leather blinkers. Eventually I made eye contact but was disappointed to get no hint of recognition. I had read about horse whispering in George Borrow's *Lavengro* not long before. I would give it a try – but got no response.

The instructor was amused. He explained that we must not lose our tempers if the ponies did not do what we wanted them to do, and we would be in real trouble if we even thought about hitting them. He began to explain how to make friends with the pit pony. But first you had to watch them as others watch hawks. The pit pony was not above screwing the stopper from your water bottle with its sensitive lips and swigging the lot if it got half a chance. If you left your sandwich tin – the sort of tin shaped like a slice from a loaf – lying about, the pony would pick it up and drop it on to the tub rails until it sprang open and it could then devour its contents. I never saw this happen but after only one day with Boxer, I could believe any story of low cunning among pit ponies.

The leather guard on the pony's head was to prevent him stunning himself on low crossbars or hanging rope pulleys. But the ponies knew their way around. We were told that if ever we got without light – *bah't leet*, that is, if your lamp went out, all you had to do was hang on to the pony's tail and tell it to go home, whereupon it would make for its stable, taking you there in relative safety. However, the pony would be extremely disappointed and reluctant to return to work when you came to an area that had lighting and it found its day's labours were not really over.

We trainee miners were in no trade union but the ponies seemed to be well organised. To protect them from the dangers of being trapped between runaway tubs there was a strong metal loop, like a link from a giant chain which hung from their harness, enclosing them front and back. This would offer protection from runaway tubs, and so on.

If for instance a tub broke loose in front and came running towards the pony, the iron loop would limit the damage to the poor creature, but even so the loop weighed what seemed to be a ton and added to the creature's burden. But in those days it was probably easier to replace a man than a pit pony. To get back to the ponies and their industrial organisation. Our instructor explained that the ponies were only allowed to pull four ten-hundredweight tubs. The ponies knew this and four tubs were all they would pull, whether empty or full. The tubs were hooked to the safety bar round the pony and then the beast was encouraged to set off. If you tried to be clever and arrange the tubs so the couplings were fully extended to prevent the pony counting the number of tubs as it set off, it would not budge. If the tubs were pushed close together so the animal could feel the weight of each tub as it began to move them, it would be happy to go, but add an extra tub and there was no way that it could be encouraged to move.

Our instructor gave us a demonstration of this. I suspect the ponies were in league with the instructors. These mentors were happy to teach us the rudiments of their trade – it was better than working, and the ponies had caught on to this as well. Pulling empty tubs all day long as we learnt the skills of horsemanship must have been much easier for them.

At the end of my day with Boxer I felt quite attached to him and was sorry to end my one and only day of a working relationship with a horse. I was sorry to leave him. I would go back up to the surface and breath God's air and see green grass, the sun, moon and stars, but Boxer would have to spend the rest of his life in the oppressive eternal darkness.

People who knew would say that it was a joyful experience to see a pit pony brought to the surface and released into green fields, never to go below again, but I was never granted this pleasure. The next day we were to learn the technique of driving a 'main and tail' engine. But that was another day so by way of a diversion, a few of us decided to go to the local cinema that night.

When we got there we found that we were not the only ones with that idea.

The pit town-type picture house audience was almost exclusively made up of Bevin Boys. I do not remember what film was showing, but what I have not forgotten is that on the newsreel there was a news item in which Mr Ernest Bevin featured prominently. Uproar broke out. Howls of derision, catcalls, rude words, and whistling created a general feeling of dissatisfaction, but no damage, no ripping up and hurling of seats as you might expect today sixty years later. The cinema manager stopped the show. He eventually got the message across that no way would the show continue unless we quietened down. He did express sympathy with our situation, but we had no right to destroy the enjoyment of the three cinema-goers present who were not Bevin Boys.

The next morning we were awakened by the cheery call of, 'Come on my lucky beauties!' We were used to it now, and swallowed our breakfast of spam and dried egg fritters. We crowded on to the coaches which took us to the pit, and half of us snatched another fifteen-minute slumber on the journey. Driving the main and tail engine was more a matter of learning and understanding the signalling system, but controlling something mechanical did not have the same challenge as persuading a wilful creature to obey your commands.

Without getting too technical, the main and tail winding engine is a stationary mechanism for rope-hauling trains – or 'runs' of full tubs along a haulage plane from the workings to the pit bottom, and for then taking them back empty. The mechanism is complicated because the return rope needs to be of variable length in order to accommodate different lengths of train. This is achieved by having two winding drums on the same driving shaft, with one that can be disconnected by means of a sort of dog clutch. It then becomes possible to widen the gap between the ends of the hauling rope and the return rope.

In this case the engine was driven by compressed air and worked very much like a steam engine. Compressed air supplied from the surface was a very useful form of power transmission. It was used in many applications, even powering light bulbs with small generators, and at the end of the line it helped with ventilation.

What we had to do was to learn the signal code so that we knew when to start the winding engine and when to stop it, or when to pay out or draw in either of the two drums. The bell was rung by an unseen entity at the other end of the line, but in our case, the instructor, who maintained an eagle-like eye on us trainees. The code was not difficult to learn and driving the engine was fun in its way. We were allowed to drive the winding engine for a couple of trips, the instructor interrupting with various bell signals to which we had to respond. Then we had to sit around while someone else had a go.

This was when I came across 'Intelligent Walt'. In our team there was a group of three boys who seemed to stick together through whatever fate threw at them. I never found out whether Walt was their mascot or their leader. Neither did I find out how he came by the name of Intelligent Walt. I suppose his parents must have christened him Walter.

It was not unusual to find mice where there were ponies. It was also an area of moral responsibility to clear up every splinter of broken glass in the event of breaking a bottle. There was no one else to do it and unseen broken glass in the darkness was a hidden menace. To lose your supply of drinking water was a tragedy. In the dust-laden atmosphere it was more precious than liquid gold.

Waiting to move on after our instruction was complete, one of our number noticed a mouse struggling with an old dirty discarded crust on a flat piece of stone. Walt decided to embark on a career of pest control. He would rid the pit of this particular rodent. He moved the stale piece of derelict sandwich to a slightly more strategic position and waited patiently for the mouse to reappear. It did. With all the speed and ferocity of a mountain lynx, Intelligent Walt struck. His choice of weapon was suspect. In the absence of anything more convenient he used his water bottle, one that when new had held a quart of Dandelion and Burdock. He was most unhappy with the derision he suffered from his friends. They would neither help him to find all the broken glass nor share their water with him. He also missed the mouse.

In the afternoons we had Theory. We were taught about miners' lamps, how gas-testing lamps worked, and the rudiments of elementary hygiene where this was virtually impossible if not non-existent. One of our teachers taught us how to spell rude words. This came about when he was encouraging us to treat our environment with respect.

The desks at which we sat had been borrowed from the Sunday school of a local chapel, or so he said. When the training scheme was over and the desks returned, he did not want any offence to be caused to delicately brought up young ladies. Could you imagine the shock they would suffer if they were to read messages carved on the desks such as 'Ernie Bevin is a...!' and worse? If we could not resist the temptation, would we please spell it right – he wanted no illiterates leaving his classroom.

There then followed a lively discussion on the spelling and etymology of a wide variety of strong language, some of the phrases I had never heard before. It was far more interesting than longwall and shortwall faces, inbyes and outbyes.

We were now in the last of our four weeks of training. The instructors were taking great delight in telling us that our holiday was nearly over. Soon we would find out what real work was like. As it happened we did – before our training was complete. It may have been part of the softening up process but we were sent out into the marshalling yard and under the hoppers which filled the railway wagons with coal for dispatch.

We had to shovel the coal which had spilled onto the ground into empty railway wagons. We had to shovel it from the uneven floor between the tracks and from between the sleepers, and then hurl it over the high sides of the wagons themselves. To move the wagons we had a long iron bar, bent and chisel-shaped at one end, which could be inserted under the wheels of the wagon. Then if two or three of us swayed on the bar, the wagon could be inched forward.

Filling these wagons was the hardest work we ever did. It was back-breaking and soul-destroying. A searingly cruel cold wind bearing wisps of snow drove in from the east. The tall lattice-girder work of the pit-head gear reached into the bleak grey sky with its spinning wheels reminding us that there were men working underground where it was warm. For the first time I wanted to be down there in the bowels of the earth.

I felt like an East European peasant scratching a meagre living from the unyielding frozen earth, the sort you would see in a German expressionist woodcut from the early twentieth century. While I thought this was degradation itself, I gave little consideration to those condemned to do this all their lives with no hope of release when the war was over.

Neither did I give a thought to others of my own age group who would, at this same time, be going through weeks of the endless mind-numbing process of square bashing in the forces. This really made us wonder why and what we were doing. At this time we had no idea where we would be sent when the month of training ended. The prospect was as depressing and bleak as the weather.

Labor Omnia Vincit

Our instructors frequently reminded us, with a detectable tinge of glee, that our 'holiday' was coming to an end. It was never fully explained to us where the instructors came from or what their qualifications were. If it was I was not listening. They were obviously 'non-productive' miners, men who had what would be now called communication skills. In all fairness I never came across any tyrants, bullies or would-be sergeant majors. Perhaps I was fortunate, but my recollections are of a group of men who could see a joke that we Bevin boys did not.

Most of us were embarking on a life that would be totally alien to our former existence. The instructors now had it easy compared with their hard working past.

When I was about five or so, my mother and father moved into a new house, a small modern semi. This was on the southern edge of the town, which was on the northern edge of the Yorkshire coalfield, approximately three miles from the city centre. The house we had lived in previously was a small stone-built terrace house, an 'improved through' as they were called in that area. It was not much more than a mile from the Town Hall – now the City Hall. The nearest expanse of grass was in a park half a mile away. On a clear Sunday, when the smoke from the mill chimneys had cleared, it was possible to see the whole black outline of Ilkley Moor, far famed in song, over the factory rooftops.

So it was a joy to move to our new home. From my back bedroom window I looked across fields and woods to a distant sky-line of the mid Pennines, complete with the masts of the BBC relay station on the high moors above Slaithwaite, a name which caused difficulties of pronunciation, and still does, for some news readers. At night for the first time I could see the stars which until then had only existed in fairy stories. My mother would take me for walks in the country lanes – sadly now built over – looking for wild flowers which I could take to school in order to enhance my chances of becoming teacher's pet. On one of these outings we suddenly encountered, round a bend in a twisting lane, an awesomely frightening figure riding a rusty, squeaking bicycle. He was black from head to foot: a dirty cloth cap, a dusty torn raincoat and muddy clogs completed the ensemble of this appalling apparition. Two sad white eyes contrasting markedly with the sombre visage beneath the neb of his tattered cap, peered wearily at us. He mumbled a friendly greeting in our direction as he pedalled along his weary way. I had never seen anybody like this before in my short existence, but in reality he looked much too tired to be truly frightening.

My mother returned his greeting and as he disappeared from sight she explained to me that he was a coal miner. She also reminded me of the working model of a colliery I had seen in a side-show at the local travelling fair. 'That is how you come home from work when you work down a coal-mine,' she added as I must have looked a bit uneasy. 'Don't worry,' she continued, 'you will never be a miner.'

My mother was much prouder than I was of my curly auburn – not ginger – hair and my delicate fair complexion. She suffered none of the taunts and jibes which were my lot at school. I got little pleasure in being compared to Little Lord Fauntleroy or being likened to Freddie Bartholomew who brought fame to the part. To be called Shirley Temple was even worse. It was only to be little more than twelve short years before my mother's assurance about my future career was to be proved so dramatically, hopelessly wrong.

But now the end of my month of training was approaching and soon I would be told that I would be allocated to a colliery where I would begin my work of *national importance*. However, if there was a pit near to my home and the manager would take me on, I would be able to work there and live at home, but there was a hint that some of the small pits on the north west fringe of the Yorkshire coalfield had gained reputations as 'hard work' pits. I never discovered what was the opposite to a hard work pit.

It just so happened that the following weekend Alf called to see me. He lived higher up the same road as I did. He was a little older than I was and already a conscripted miner. He had been a painter and decorator before serving his country underground. I had seen Alf about but did not really know him. Alf had heard that I was in training to be a miner and dropped in to offer advice. He suggested that I should apply to the manager of his colliery which was only about five miles away. He pulled no punches – it was a hard work pit – its name? Nutter Lane! But what the hell? I could become a nutter and live at home which would make up for a lot. Anyway I think Alf wanted company going to work on the cold dark mornings.

I went to see the manager and to see what the mine looked like from the outside. It was not big, employing about 150 men and about 300 foot deep. I was directed to the manager's office. He was a big man for a small pit. His face shouted experience. He was gruff and unlikely to stand up with any nonsense – but there may have been a deeply hidden hint of compassion and even understanding of the human condition which belied his forbidding exterior.

The interview was short. He looked me up and down, sighed, turned away, gazed out of the grimy office window and stared at the spinning pit-head wheels for a few seconds, which to me seemed an eternity. Then he looked at me again and, with an air of weary resignation, asked the rhetorical question – why was he obliged to employ Bevin Boys? Yes, I could start on Monday. It would be surface work for the first fortnight, he reminded me. If I had a pair of old leather gloves it would be a good idea to bring them.

Alf called again to see how I had got on at my interview. He thought he could give me more helpful hints and tips about my new place of work. He began by telling me that the first two weeks on the surface would be tough and before the end I would not be able to wait to get underground. He recounted how at the end of his first week, five and a half days as it was then, he had gone home on the Saturday afternoon, straight to bed, and did not wake up again until it was time to go back to work on the following Monday morning. All this was very encouraging.

It turned out that he did not exaggerate.

In the following months and years, I was to get to know and admire Alf. He had qualities which I was never to possess. Above all he had a quickness of thought and a rapier-like wit which I could only envy.

I presented myself at the colliery on the Monday, only to be told that I did not have to start until Tuesday. I felt a bit of an idiot, there in my new working clothes. I had the safety hat, Toetector boots – complete with shiny steel toe caps, and a pair of overalls. I felt very conspicuous – like the well-known sore thumb. 'You might as well have a look round, seeing you are here,' I was told. This small pit had one manager and three deputies, of which one worked mostly nights on maintenance work. The manager was proud of the fact that this was a modern pit – all electric. But there was not much for the electricity to power – just the pit-head winding engine and a main and tail haulage engine at the pit bottom. This was driven by a man who held deputy's papers but was not employed as such. On the surface there was an 'endless rope-haulage' system which took the full tubs from the pit bank to the screening shed, where there was a crushing machine also driven by a powerful electric motor.

Down below there were no power cutters. The coal was 'hand got' from the seam which varied between twenty inches and approximately twenty-six inches.

At the moment I was more concerned about how I was to be employed on the surface. It was explained that I would be mostly working on the screens, but at times I would be tramming waste from the pit-head to the waste heap. I was taken to see the screening shed. This was where the upcoming coal was sorted and graded.

In this case the working area was in a large ramshackle wooden structure with a corrugated tin roof. Underneath this area were the hoppers holding the sorted coal ready to be dropped into the vehicles used to take it to its ultimate destination. Even though the colliery grounds were bounded on one side by a railway line, there was no connection to this main-line artery. The screens were at the top of a slope fed by tubs pulled by the endless rope from the pit-head. It was unusual that the screening area was on a level higher than the pit-head, but this was because the pit itself was on a sloping site. More usually the pit bank is on a higher level so the raised coal finds its way to the screens and delivery point by gravity. Here things were different. The tubs, which each held five hundredweight of coal, were up-ended in a tippler to shower their contents on to the screens. These were sheets of steel one above the other, set at contrasting angles, and with progressively larger holes in them. The largest was in the top sheet, the smallest in the bottom. These screens were constantly shaken backwards and forwards by another electric motor. The coal was either sifted according to size through the holes, or fell off the sides and into the appropriate hoppers. About four people worked on the screens. Their work was to pick out any stone that came up with the coal, and shovel it through the crusher. This is where I realised the truth of the manager's recommendation that I should have some old leather gloves.

The crusher fed the produce of its toil into a separate hopper. The resulting dust was sold as ninety percent combustible boiler fuel.

Who were we to complain? There was a roof to this primitive structure but no windows, just open spaces, and the keen withering east wind offered no comfort as it blasted through. This was where I would work for the next two weeks. These were to be the worst two weeks of my working life.

I was told to report for work the following morning at, or just before 7 a.m. This was the time the screens began their remorseless shuffle. Now I saw the wisdom of the old leather gloves. As the coal came shuttering down in its merry dance, it required some manual dexterity to seize the lumps of stone without getting fingers trapped or nipped in the melee of sliding coal. I took my place at the screens and began this mind-numbing, monotonous work. I found myself working opposite a character known simply as Old Tom. Nobody knew how old he was. He was not a big man but apparently had been a sailor who had trained in sail. He spoke but little. He was impervious to cold. In the most bitter weather he would still work in shirt sleeves. If you passed comment on the freezing weather conditions he would say that he could believe that it was cold. There was no seniority or indeed any pecking order, but it was accepted that nobody caused any offence to Old Tom. However, I was the new lad and in some way at the bottom of the heap.

We all took bottles of tea – without milk – made or 'mashed' just before leaving home for work and just enough to fill a quart mineral water bottle. The heat from this bottle would keep us warm on the way to work. On arrival at the pit we would venture into the air-raid shelter for a few minutes before starting work. This was a stout brick-built cavern beneath the main pit-head configuration. There was always a warm cheery fire in a grate like those found outside a watchman's hut.

Here we would arrange our bottles in a neat semicircle in front of the warm fire – there was no shortage of coal here – but if there was to be any preference, Tom's bottle was to be nearest to the fire.

Belonging to the new lad, my bottle would be farthest from the fire. In spite of his apparent resistance to cold, old Tom always wanted his bottle to be full of warm tea. There was a break at 11 a.m. when the screens were stopped for twenty minutes. Then we would retire to the air-raid shelter to eat our 'bread' and drink our tea. Here our snack was always known as bread, not snap or bait as at other places. My curiosity was never roused sufficiently for me to find out why. About half way between starting and bread-time it was my privilege to run down from the screens to the air-raid shelter to rotate Old Tom's bottle in order to make sure it was nice and warm for his break. For me this was a welcome respite from the tedium of sorting coal. Even when working full out it was bitterly cold. Now I found out why the naked electric light bulbs, although hanging in an atmosphere of stone and coal dust, were always relatively clean. They provided a source of warmth for frozen fingers. The hoppers into which the coal fell after sorting had flat bottoms with traps in them. There was no such refinement as sloping sides. Therefore it was necessary that somebody had to climb down into the hopper and encourage the coal to fall through the square openings into the wagons waiting beneath. This work was both dirty and dangerous in the extreme.

It needed an eye on the coal falling into the hopper all the time to avoid being hit by a falling piece of coal, and what air there was, was almost unbreathable. I never got as dirty underground as when working in these unforgiving hell holes.

The prospects of spending two weeks in these conditions became unthinkable. Now my conscience pricks me, looking back to those distant days. In my innocence I never really gave a thought to my companions condemned to spend the rest of their working days in these dreadful conditions. I had the comfort of the knowledge that eventually I would be released from this form of industrial slavery but only God knew when that would be.

The other aspect of surface work was emptying waste stone on to the pit hill. As the pit was on the slope of a hillside, the waste could be taken straight from the pit-head out on a level tramway to the edge of the pit stack and tipped down the side. There was no aerial flight or any other ingenious system to build up the waste heap. The stone was pushed out in the standard five-hundredweight tubs. Because the stone was approximately twice as heavy as coal, it was just about necessary for two men to push and tipple the heavy tubs. It still took a lot of effort for two men to up-end the tub, even though it was partly balanced on its short wheelbase. On top of all this, it took quite a bit of skill to get the tub to tip its contents without losing it and letting it go hurtling down the steep hillside.

I began to learn the knack of dealing with heavy weights such as I would never have thought that I could possibly move by myself, although it did take a lot of learning.

I was slightly less than normal build, but reasonably robust. I never thought of myself as a Charles Atlas. I had passed my medical as A1. My father had pointed out that the only reason you went for a medical was to determine whether you went into the army or the ATS.

I did just about survive my first two weeks of surface work and could not wait to get underground. For one thing, underground work finished half an hour earlier than the surface work. It was not as dirty, and it was not as cold. Even so we did not go home clean. This was during wartime and the men had been previously offered the choice of pit-head baths or a canteen. They wisely chose the canteen. This gave them an extra main meal in times of rationing. It was cosy, warm and comfortable. The ladies who ran the canteen always put on a good meal – as I have already stated pit-head canteen tea was the best in the world – and these ladies were always homely and cheerful.

It was a relief to get underground. I had never been as dirty in my short life as during the period of my surface work. The dirt was never easy to get rid of. We had no shower at home – few people did in those days. The bath had to be filled twice to get clean. Anybody who has gone through this sort of experience will regard with some suspicion the old adage 'Where there's muck, there's money'. I was daily enveloped in all this muck but there was little evidence of any money. When I asked where the money was I was always told, 'up at the big house in the trees at the top of the hill.' This was where the owning family lived. At this time I began to entertain doubts about the 'dignity of honest toil.' Whoever thought that one up was unlikely to have experienced the dignity of the toil which now claimed my working hours.

This labour had almost conquered me, but not quite. After what seemed an eternity my two weeks on the surface came to an end. On the last day at bread-time the manager came looking for me. 'Get your 'at, lad and come wi' me,' was his curt greeting. He took me to the lamp room and introduced me to the lamp room keeper, telling him to give me a lamp. The keeper gave me a cap lamp and a tally, no. 64. In future I would get this tally every day – a metal disc a little bit larger than an old imperial penny, but with a hole at the top. This I had to take down the pit every time I went down and hang it on a board with rows of numbered cuphooks. At the end of every shift I had to take it back with my lamp to the lamp room and hand it in. This was how they kept a check on who was down below and who wasn't.

I girded my loins with my belt and battery and followed the manager to the top of the shaft. The manager was gruff, but not entirely unfriendly. I was privileged to be making my first descent with him. The cage would hold two five-hundredweight tubs, one on a hinged flap above the other. When used for 'man riding' the flap would be raised into the vertical position and then four men could stand in the same place. There were removable gates to prevent the men from falling out, but when winding coal these were removed completely. So this was where my privilege lay – riding with the manager – during an unscheduled break in the coal winding day – in a cage without gates. He advised me to hold tight, but I needed no telling. He watched me all the way down, more to see my reactions to this hairy ride than to make sure I held tight.

This was a much more gentle and slower ride than the descent at the training colliery. We got to the bottom. 'Right lad, you'll do, you are down my pit now!' And so my underground career began.

Nutter Lane, the pit where the author worked
Author's sketch

A Man Could Stand Up

I did not know how to regard the manager. All these years later I now realise he wasn't really a bad sort of chap, but the way we saw him was as an official, a boss in charge of an organisation which employed conscripted labour. Someone to be treated with suspicion. Even so it was not to be very long before I discovered the basic rule in mining, the rule which bound us all together, man and management, in a form of trust and comradeship. In training we had been told of many underground regulations but the basic rule was, do something wrong and you get hurt. It was as simple as that.

On my first day underground at the new pit, the manager, Mr Carlton, told me I was going to begin by helping a by-worker who was busy driving a new heading not far from the pit bottom. I was soon to find out that although Bob was the manager's name, he liked his proper title. We all called him Bob but not to his face. Wilf was the name of the by-worker. He was drilling a hole in the rock at the end of a short low tunnel with a hand drill. 'I've got a new lad to give you a bit of a hand, Wilf,' began the manager by way of an introduction. 'He is another Bevin Boy; his name is Reggie.'

My heart sank even deeper in the Stygian gloom. Wilf was a hard looking man, all muscle and sinew, bright blue eyes shining out of his toil-worn craggy miner's face. He wore two leather straps, like watch straps, each without a watch on his wrists. These gave him greater strength he was to tell me later.

When the manager said my name was Reggie, I broke in with 'No it's not, my name is John,' (my second name) 'or Jonty if you like.' This had no effect. It was going to be Reggie no matter how much I protested.

I had always been self-conscious about my name. It must have been a trendy name in the roaring twenties when I first appeared in this mortal vale of tears. I suffered for it at school, and not just from my fellow school children. I still cringe when I recall our woodwork master, basically a kindly old soul in secondary school who reminded me a bit of Stanley Holloway. At our first woodwork lessons, he would introduce us to new tools and to make sure we remembered the names, he used the following formula. He would hold, for example, a spokeshave and say to us, 'This is a spokeshave, boys. What is it called?' We would then chorus in unison, 'A spokeshave, Sir.' Woe betide anybody who did not make the required reply – a sharp clout on the ear was the reward.

One day Old Man Ellis, as we affectionately got to know him, produced a brand new gleaming, shining, metal Stanley Jack plane – a bit of a triumph in wartime. 'This, boys, is a Jack plane. What is it called?' We all made the necessary reply. The next question was a rhetorical one. 'Why is it called a Jack plane?' We all stood in ignorant unresponsive silence. 'I will tell you, boys. You will see that it is larger and stronger than a smoothing plane. It is for tackling long large pieces of wood. It is for doing hard work, a man's work; that is why it is called a Jack plane. It would be useless to call it a Reginald plane!'

Back to the underground scene where I was suffering further embarrassment over my unfortunate name.

'Nay,' the manager chipped in. 'We haven't got a "Reggie" down this pit – Reggie it'll have to be.' So Reggie it was. 'Wilf will tell you what to do for just now. I'll come and take you to the main face tomorrow,' he continued.

I got on all right with Wilf. The immediate task was boring a shot hole with a hand drill. Wilf began to explain how the hand drill worked. The drill had a handle and a lever, each with a ratchet on the end of the drill shaft. This was held by an adjustable stand in a position parallel to the roof and at right angles to the face it was to drill. Because there was not much room, neither the handle nor the drill could make a complete revolution, so we had to push and pull alternately until the bit had penetrated the stone to a sufficient depth. It took a lot of effort. I was intrigued to see that Wilf was collecting the dust which dropped from the drill hole on sheets of old newspaper that had been used to bring in his sandwiches. Then he carefully wrapped the dust up in rolls about six to eight inches long and about an inch in diameter. Curiosity got the better of me; I had to ask why. He looked at me as if I was completely green, which, of course, I was. After a couple of seconds mulling it over he told me that these paper rolls were for shoving in the hole to hold the explosive in place when the deputy came to fire the shot.

This was real excitement. First day underground and I was involved in explosives. The deputy came. Wilf told him I was the new lad and that my name was Reggie. The deputy said he would remember that. And he did. He looked at the work, shoved the explosive and detonator into the hole we had just drilled and told us to find a place of safety.

We hid in a refuge hole and the deputy then uncoiled a length of wire and connected it to his shot-firing battery. Then he made a couple of tests for gas. 'Right!' he said. There was a hell of a bang and the gate we were in was filled with smoke, choking dust and what the miners called 'reek'. It was difficult to breathe, but eventually the three of us, the deputy, Wilf and myself crawled back to see the damage.

'Fine, that's okay,' was the verdict as we surveyed the pile of shattered stone. The two men took great delight in explaining that it was now my job to shovel all of this into the awaiting tub and push it to the pit bottom. I began this task, which was not easy in the confined, cramped space where we were. Wilf broke in, 'Nay, Reggie lad, I'll give thee a hand. T'stone's twice as heavy as coal, we'll shift this together!' I was very grateful for his help. I felt more grateful to him when he told me that this was the last tub of the shift, and we would soon be able to go home.

We walked to the pit bottom and Wilf asked me how my first day underground had gone. I was tired and disappointed when I found that I was not to work with Wilf the next day. In fact I never did again. Even though it was mid-January and bitterly cold I was glad to get to the surface after my first working day underground.

There were few accidents at this little pit, but to return to the surface in one piece was always a relief that never faded. However, I was by no means the only one to be suffering this culture shock, this dramatic change in lifestyle – especially getting up in the middle of the night. The next day I was to start work as what the manager called a 'trammer'.

In a lot of collieries I would have been called a 'putter', but here all the miners, sticking to the tradition of the area, called us 'hurriers'. They also called the tubs we had to push 'corves', no doubt related to the German word *Korb* meaning basket, a memory of the times when coal was brought out in baskets. The work of a trammer, the manager had explained, was to bring the coal in tubs from the face to the pass-by where they were made up into trains or runs and hauled to the pit bottom. He took some pleasure in explaining that the workings were two low for pit ponies, and that was why he employed Bevin Boys.

The manager said he would see me at the pit bottom the next day and take me in to the district where I would work. This was about a mile and a half walk from the pit bottom, not an easy walk for, apart from the first 200 yards or so, there were few places where a man could stand up. He met me and told me to follow him in. This was easier said than done. He had what he called his 'flat tram', a beloved little vehicle, not much more than a few boards mounted on four tub wheels, just big enough for him to kneel on. He used a high candle-power hand lantern, which he held between his knees as he coasted along, occasionally pushing himself along with one leg. It was amazing the speed he could get up to, particularly if the haulage rope was running. Then he would grab hold of that and by a series of sharp tugs on the travelling rope would gain a fantastic speed. There was no keeping up with him.

He did stop once or twice to make sure I was still there and to point out things of interest. At one place he told me that we were going through the 'pillar'. This was an area where the coal had been left in place to support the foundations of an old hall on the surface which played a significant part in one of the Brontë novels – *Shirley* I think it was. 'You look the sort of lad who might be able to read. Do you know owt about these Brontës?' he asked. I wasn't sure what sort of reply he wanted. I told him that I had not lived long enough yet to have finished anything by the weird sisters of Haworth, but I had seen Laurence Olivier and Merle Oberon in *Wuthering Heights* and that people I knew in Haworth said that heather never grew as high as it did in that film.

Next he pointed out the first-aid and fire station, as if to reassure me. It was just the end of an old heading that had been filled in. There was a stretcher and a box with a red cross symbol on it. There was also an ingenious battery-operated gadget for relighting oil lamps without sending them to the surface, but it never worked. Eventually we got to the face. The system in this pit was the 'short wall' system where each man worked about ten yards of coal-face, with 'gates' leading from each face to a transverse 'crossgate' which in turn led to the main pass-by. The seam was about twenty-two to twenty-six inches (fifty to sixty centimetres) high and the gates themselves a little over three feet high.

Fred Wakeman was the first collier I was to work for and I was introduced to him again as 'the only Reggie in the pit'. Fred was a quiet sort of man, a local councillor, and a tidy worker – he always swept his particular work area clean at the end of his shift. He accepted me with patience. I did not know that he was one of the more productive men and I did not know how much coal he was going to get and how many tubs I would be expected to fill and shove to the pass-by.

The gates from the face to the crossgate were both low and narrow. As time passed and the face advanced from the crossgate, the sides began to close in. The stone had razor-sharp edges which were particularly cruel to a novice like myself. While the air in this pit was cleaner and colder than it had been in my training colliery, there seemed to be far less room. There were not as many men about and consequently fewer points of light which indicated human activity.

So it was that I began to have fears that I might not survive in my new subterranean surroundings. It was hard work. It was dark with little sense of direction, and I never knew what time it was. The work was all hand work. The colliers had no machinery; all the coal was hand got as they said. At the end of the shift Fred had cut enough coal to fill fourteen tubs. Each tub held five hundredweight so that was three and half tons between us. At the end of the shift I was absolutely jiggered. 'Tha's done a good day's work, lad. I hope Ah gets thee again,' he told me as I got ready for the long walk out. I found out later that while the coal getters were on piece-work, they had to fill at least eight tubs per shift to get the 'guaranteed' wage of £5 per week. It was wartime and everybody was encouraged to do the best they could and piece work was a good incentive. So Fred was doing his bit, setting a good example and also enhancing his own paypacket.

Talking to other lads at the pit bottom they acknowledged that I had done a fair day's work. I had managed fairly well. I had not yet suffered any damage. I had been warned that I would have a sore back for the first few months, and this would not be caused by hard work. What the trammer had to learn was that in the low narrow gates he had to keep his back down – not arch it as he heaved and shoved the loaded tubs.

It took me a surprisingly long time to learn. You would think the first time you took the skin off the nobbles of your spine that would be a good enough lesson, but no, in the heat of frustration when trying to push reluctant tubs uphill, I did it time and time again. I was not the only one to do this. It seemed to happen to everybody when they first started. Like most things, there is a knack to be learned.

While the work never became easy, after the first few months I found that it was not as much of a struggle as it had been at first and I was not skinning my spine quite as much.

On the way out I met my new found friend Alf, the lad who lived in the same street as I did. He wanted to know how I had got on, particularly if I still had skin on the nobbles of my backbone. The answer to this was 'very little'. He was encouraging in an inverted sort of way and explained that the work might get easier, if I could get used to it. But I must never let them 'put on me'. It seems I had done a good day's work, but it took a long time for it to begin to get easier. I looked at Alf. He was not much bigger than me, a little taller, but about the same weight. I had noticed him at work and had seen that he managed to throw the loaded tubs about much more easily than I could. 'You'll learn,' he told me and warned me to keep my hands below the top edge of the tubs or I would have no skin on my knuckles either. I was beginning to find out what it was like to work in a real man's world and I wasn't all that impressed.

During the first week or two I would get home, make myself a cup of tea – no instant coffee then, and fall asleep stretched out on the floor. My mother wasn't keen on me flaking out in her best chairs.

Alternatively I would sink into the bath and fall asleep there, only to be woken up when the water got cold. We had a white cat called Blanche and on one occasion I fell asleep on my back on the floor in front of the fire. In the midst of my exhausted slumber the cat recognised my supine stomach as a warm and suitable place to share my sleep. There were not many warm car bonnets so beloved of cats where we lived in those days, so I suppose she took me for a good supine substitute. As it happens she must have eaten something which did not agree with her – she suddenly developed a fit of hiccups. The entire force of her first violent spasm was transmitted to my recumbent solar plexus. My time in the mine had already made me nervous of any unexpected sudden movement. My reaction was as swift as it was automatic. Instinctively expecting the roof to come in, I was up and on my knees snaking for the door at a speed that would have put a bat out of hell to shame. The poor cat was marginally quicker. Like an unavoidable streak of greased lightning accompanied by a screaming squawk such as you would hear at a concert of modern avant-garde music given by an unenthusiastic orchestra, she shot out of the back door just as my mother came in.

It took a while to convince my mother that I was not tormenting the poor creature in an effort to get it to leave home. It was a nice cat as cats went in those days. Eventually I did not need to sleep so long as I gradually got used to my daily exhaustion, but I still did not like getting up in the middle of the night, nor did I ever really get used to it.

The Hand of God

After a couple of months my muscles were beginning to harden up. I was beginning to manage the tubs with a little more skill, and while the work was no easier, I was managing my energy resources a little better. I was now learning the idiosyncrasies of these devilish little coal tubs. To an onlooker they all looked alike but they had character if not personality. The older they were, the more easily they ran and took less effort to push. Apart from a small number of metal ones which were extremely unpopular, they were made by the colliery blacksmith.

Two stout beams provided a chassis and dumb buffers, with crosspieces forming the wooden floor which was surmounted by sides and ends. The whole structure was bound with iron edges and corner plates to form a rugged conveyance for the black diamonds. At one end of the chassis was a hook, at the other was a short coupling chain. This meant that all the tubs had to be of the same orientation otherwise they could not be linked together to form a train, or run. If one was brought out the wrong way round it caused a lot of trouble. The running gear consisted of two axles with four cast-iron wheels with curvy spokes. These ran in plain bearings; roller bearings were impractical, largely because of the penetrating dust which had similar properties to Carborundum. The gauge of the track was approximately twenty-two inches. In practice this was the length from the tip of my left elbow to the tip of my middle finger, plus the spread fingers of my right hand (seventeen inches plus five inches), something I have never forgotten and often found useful in later life when it has been necessary to measure when no ruler was available.

Between the tracks of the main road to the pit bottom there were some lubricant injectors which squirted a dose of tub fat onto the axles every time a full tub passed over them. This evil substance was supposed to make the tubs run more easily, but as it appeared to be a mixture of black treacle, coal tar and instant glue, it was more likely to slow them down. Its adhesive properties were such that if you got it on your skin you were marked for life. The size of the tubs was such that they held approximately five hundredweight of coal, or, when used to make up a Paddy Mail train, two men could sit in one side by side, and possibly a third if he sat crosswise with his knees tucked under his chin. But more of that later. In handling these tubs we Bevin Boys had to push the full ones – 'fulluns' – from the coal-face to the main pass-by and take the empties back. As it was all single track, it was inevitable that you would meet somebody coming in the opposite direction. This meant that the empty tub had to give way to the full one. The empty had to be tipped on its side in the narrow confines of the crossgate. This could be done at the end of a gate that led to the coal-face or occasionally, but rarely, in a space where the crossgate was a little bit wider. An old pit-prop laid at the side of the track made this easier. But it was always another chore having to tip up a tub like this, although it often gave an opportunity for a bit of gossip at the point of passing.

So that the tubs could be identified and credited to the collier who had filled them, there was a small hole at each end to enable an identifying tag to be attached.

At our pit these tallies were known as 'motties' or 'dommies', I don't know the derivation of these words. The tallies were made of cast iron, either triangular or in the form of a circular disc with a number cast on them. A loop of strong string enabled them to be fastened to the tub. Each collier had his own number. This system avoided chalking the number on the tub which always caused a lot of problems. It was difficult to rub off the chalk. At the pit-head each tub was weighed and credited to the appropriate coal getter by the check weighman, so that his pay could be worked out. Putting your own number on another's tub was the worst crime that anyone could commit – it would almost lead to a lynching. In order to check the check weighman, a democratically elected member of the work-force sat at his side to make sure that the records he kept were correct.

The colliers had their own equipment: basically a pick, a shovel, a hammer, a piece of chalk, a supply of motties, and of course, a lamp. We trammers just had a lamp. The colliers worked in a narrow seam, (twenty-two inches to twenty-six inches) their working space was very restricted. The picks were small compared with those used by navvies. The shaft would be about thirty inches long and the blade was about eighteen inches from point to point. Each man would have several blades, each with his own number engraved on it, so he could leave the blunt ones with the blacksmith at the end of the shift to be sharpened for the following day. The hammers and shovels were short-shafted for work in confined spaces. It is possible to gain some idea of the working space by lying underneath a dining room table pushed up against a wall and then imagining the wall is the coal-face.

Sometimes the coal was hard, sometimes it was soft, but mostly it was hard, not quite as hard as diamond, but you could believe it was. I spent almost three years providing motive power for coal tubs. I have never worked out how much coal I shifted during that time, or the amount of sweat that I generated. But the sweat was a variable factor. In the first months I would sweat a lot; the sweat would mingle with tears of frustration when the only purpose in life became the necessity to shove nearly six unwilling hundredweight of coal and tub up these narrow black gates. I began to learn something of the innate animosity of inanimate objects, brooding there with deeply hidden malice. I forgot all about the sun, blue skies, rain, ice, frost, snow sludge, and everything else. My only reason for being was just to shift coal, my very existence a mad frantic determination, as every sinew, muscle and bone in my body strove to get these tubs up the severe gradients to the pass-by. I never stopped to think why I was doing it – basically because I had to – but I did sometimes wonder why horses take part in races. They don't stop to wonder why they are doing it, but enthusiasts say that the horses enjoy racing. I have yet to read a racing correspondent quoting a winner telling how much it enjoyed the race.

But the work did get easier, or at least I eventually became as deft as the others at handling these tubs and did not need to put quite as much effort into it. Eventually I fell into the ways of the others and was able to lead a normal sort of life out of working hours.

There was no easy work and as every trammer dreamt of tubs

with free-running bearings, the collier dreamt of being in a seam of soft coal.

Of course the hardness of the coal did vary, but it was mostly hard. The colliers had either electric lanterns or oil lamps to work with. The electric lanterns were heavy but reliable. The oil lamps were lighter and gave a softer light. They were slightly different to the normal oil lamp in that the flame burnt in a glass funnel inside the outer glass. They had a corrugated radiator round the top of the gauze chamber and gave off a fair bit of warmth. The older coal getters liked the oil lamps, but for some, it had been necessary to provide a doctor's certificate to get an electric lamp.

The mobile workers were given cap lamps. These fitted on to the safety helmets, which in those days – the 1940s – were not compulsory, but highly recommended. Most of the colliers preferred to wear an old flat cap. Some of the more fashion-conscious would favour a beret worn at a rakish angle or on the back of the head, like Gracie Fields. The cap lamp had a heavy battery which hung on your belt with a leather pad to stop it rubbing on your back too much. Some were fortunate enough to have these pads made in a sort of box shape in which the battery would sit. If the battery should leak, these boxes prevented the acid from running down your back and to such a location that it would cause extreme discomfort.

Occasionally we trammers would have to work with oil lamps. This was if we were the last to arrive at the pit before they stopped winding men, and all the cap lamps had been given out to the early birds. Working with an oil lamp meant that you had to have something to hang it on. The lamp had to hang from the neck, as your legs got in the way if you hung it on your belt and it was too hot for that anyway.

Some miners wore dog-collars, but a stout neckerchief tied securely round the neck did the job. The big problem with the oil lamp was that a sudden knock could deck it out and as this was a schedule A pit, the lamp had to be sent to the surface to be re-lit. In the underground fire station there was an ingenious gadget that could relight an oil lamp without it having to be opened. It contained a heavy battery and could cause a spark across an electrode above the wick in the lamp, but more often than not the battery was flat. If you lost your light you were then in the state of being *Bah't leet* – not always an un-enviable position since you could not work and so had a welcome sit-down until your lamp was replaced. Among a group of conscientious workers like ourselves, I find it difficult to believe that any one of us would even think about accidentally putting his lamp out.

The deputies had gas testing lamps. These were equipped with a built-in relighting system, something like the flint and wheel you would find in a cigarette lighter. This was necessary because when testing for gas, sometimes a mini-explosion would take place inside the lamp itself, extinguishing the light. These lamps burnt with an orange glow different to the normal working lights and it was easy to recognise the deputies from a distance by the colour of the light from their lamps. The deputies had both oil lamps and a cap lamp, but the manager had a high candle-power lamp. This projected a searingly brilliant beam of incandescent white light which nearly burnt out the back of your eyes if you were so unlucky as to look directly at it.

I don't think the manager hated us as much as he tried to make out. He would frequently stop to talk to us when he came on his rounds. He would express some sympathy with us for having to leave cissy jobs to come and do a man's work. After all there was a war on. He would suggest that we took up some intellectual pursuit to keep our minds active like learning to play chess, or stamp collecting, or he would tell us how easy we had it compared with when he was a lad. In the days of his youth the tubs had no wheels, the mine was half-flooded and he had to work sixteen hours a day and shovel the coal with his bare hands.

On one occasion three or four of us were having our snap-break. Everybody was allowed twenty minutes, but we had become so absorbed in the glittering intellectual content of our conversation that we did not notice the swift passage of time. We were suddenly surprised by the manager who sprang upon us as we sat huddled together at the end of an old gate. He tapped his watch menacingly. He and the deputies had pocket watches in shockproof cases which made them almost the size of an alarm clock. We politely enquired after his well-being in the forlorn hope that this might dispel his look of barely suppressed anger.

He looked at us all, and emphatically tapped his watch again. 'There has been somebody sat in this gate for nearly forty minutes!' My quick-thinking friend Alf looked him calmly in the eye and said, with immense confidence, 'No, there hasn't.'

With ill-concealed impatience, the manager then explained, 'I have been sat just round the corner with my light switched off, timing them,' again tapping his watch. Alf countered this with, 'You must be mistaken, Mr Carlton. We have been here for forty-five minutes and we haven't seen a single soul.' Mr Carlton looked at Alf in disbelief, retreated in silence, put his watch away, and stormed off into the darkness.

We did not see him for another week. This sort of thing is now known as the put down but Alf always thought of it as a 'fitting up', a skill which I admired in Alf but was never able to equal.

Often the snap-breaks were quite enjoyable particularly with some of the full-time miners. Their conversation would cover a wide range of subjects. Some of these men were very public-minded and served as local councillors, others were very well read as they used to say, but it was a perpetual source of wonder to me that no matter what the subject of discussion may have been at the beginning, it always finished up on one of the many fascinating facets of sex.

One of these colliers came to be known as Pudpil. Alf and I came from a place called Bierley – so Pudpil would call us the Bierley Buggers. His home was in Pudsey and it was generally acknowledged that he was a bit of a pillock, so Alf and I named him Pudpil, a name which stuck to him like glue. For all that he was a likeable good-natured sort of chap. He claimed to have seen every known animal in the act of sexual congress. Challenges to this staggering claim led to some very interesting, often exciting, snap-time philosophical discussions.

Among the colliers we had to work for was a lay preacher, John Murgatroyd, a devout sort of man who never swore. In all fairness to him despite all our taunts he never tried to convert or save us. If a piece of loose rock fell on his toe or other extremity, 'Flipping Heck' would be the response.

We would ask him why he did not come out with a more

robust expression of displeasure – usually beginning with the same initials, because that was what he really meant. 'This would be a sin,' would be his usual reply. We would counter by asking if the sin was not in the thought, rather than the actual words, and was this surely not a greater sin, conveying a false impression to his less disciplined colleagues? These taunts never affected John and he never seemed to think any the worse of us. On one occasion he told us that he had a book at home that had a photograph of Noah's Ark in it. We questioned the veracity of this. One of our little group thought that it was some time after Noah that the photographic process was invented. But no, John had this book with a photograph of Noah's Ark in it. One bright spark asked if it showed any kangaroos. Someone else asked if it was not an artist's impression, but again no, John was having none of this. It was a photograph. When we demanded to know how it could possibly be a photograph we were reminded that the Almighty was all powerful and could do anything. If He wanted a photograph to illustrate this book, He would arrange for a photograph to be a available. Some of us were impressed by his faith and others were less charitable. As our break was coming to an end nobody provoked any further discussion. We went about our work older and wiser men.

I was privileged to witness an example of divine intervention. I was working in a district known as the Old Three South. This was one some way off the route of the main haulage plain and because of a geological fault had some steep inclines.

The pass-by where the runs of full tubs were made up was some distance from the main road and at right angles to it. While the pass-by was double-tracked, the point where it became single on the way out was very narrow and it became obvious that it was getting narrower. This was probably due to some shifting ground, perhaps due to the fault. But every few days a by-worker had to come and spend some time chipping away at the advancing side wall.

One day the by-worker was a man called John Rigg. John was of larger build than the average miner but was one of those men who seemed to be completely at home underground, as if they had been created there and had never had normal birth and childhood. He wore his hard hat back to front because the neb restricted his vision. He had sized up the situation and was busily cutting away at the threatening rock when the manager came along with three mining students from the local university. His visit coincided with our snap-break and we were sat on the outbye side of the hazard which John was correcting. John had a lot of instinctive knowledge about the underground world and the manager obviously respected this. He was regaling us with entertaining experiences from his past when the visitors arrived. The manager explained to the students what the problem was and that John was his most experienced by-worker. To emphasise his confidence he asked John to explain how much rock was in danger of collapsing and blocking the entire pass-by. John's reply was brief and to the point. 'There is only one who knows the answer to that!' The manager looked at him for a couple of seconds, then, 'And who might that be, John?'

John, who was one who enjoyed chewing tobacco, paused, released an amount of well-chewed tobacco juice with confident aim narrowly missing the manager and said, 'God all bloody mighty!'

What surprised me was how quickly these inexperienced mining engineering students could run in the confined space of the haulage road. They were almost as quick as the manager and the rest of us, to recognise the Supreme Being's response to John's blasphemic taunt in the creaking and rumblings of the surrounding rock as an unspecified tonnage of rock collapsed and filled the outward end of the pass-by with a certainty that suggested the influence of a guiding hand. It took over six weeks to get that pass-by working again. Nobody was injured and the men who were working at the face a hundred yards away were able to get out via the ventilation route. Regrettably, nothing in this actually convinced me of the existence of a divine providence.

And so life went on. Would the war never end? And if it did would we recruits be released immediately from our industrial slavery?

To See Ourselves as Others See Us...

Not the least of the problems which beset the Bevin Boy beginning his new career were those of social distinction. In the days when class and position appeared to be more important than earning power, 'respectable' people did not mine coal for a living even though it was an industry of great national importance. This was not of so much concern to me as much as it was to a number of relatives, a situation not entirely uncommon among other mining conscripts. After the first saunter home down the street in working clothes for all to see my embarrassment soon wore off.

At the training colliery I had been given a safety hat, a pair of working boots – Toetectors, boots reinforced with a steel toecap, and issued with extra clothing coupons. After a few weeks I fell into the dress code of my colleagues. We would leave our hard hats underground before we came out of the pit and would sport either a cloth cap or a more stylish beret. At first flannel shirts were acceptable work wear but it soon became apparent that the fashion-conscious trammer would wear an old football strip – from which team was not critical – but this did add a brief splash of colour to our drab subterranean surroundings. For trammers it was essential to wear the shirt or strip outside trousers, which were very often corduroy, with belt and lamp battery outside. This made sure that grit and stone which fell on your back did not get wedged between belt and skin, with consequent disastrously uncomfortable abrasive results.

Some coal getters wore their shirts outside like this for the very same reason and this code of dress brought disaster to one vociferous collier noted for his enthusiasm, tidiness and gift for a picturesque description of anything untoward. Jim Newton had found himself in a seam of soft coal and had stayed on to the last minute. He had filled the last of many tubs for the day. Before leaving he had gone along his face, setting the regulation number pit-props in the twenty-two inch seam to preserve safety during

65

the night. Doubled up on himself he hammered home his last prop about six feet away from his exit gate, hurled his hammer towards the gate end where his jacket and other possessions were, and made an attempt to straighten up in order to crawl out. Then it was that he discovered fate had struck a cruel blow. Jim could not move. He had set his last prop on his shirt tail. He was irrevocably secured near the coal-face. He tried shouting but everybody else had been more eager than he was to leave. His cries went unheeded. It was not until the deputy, who checked the tally board, saw that Jim's tally had not been collected that he was missed. After asking around he found that no one had seen Jim leave and so realised something was wrong.

It was a very disgruntled deputy who had to go all the way back to the coal-face and search for Jim. The winding engine man wasn't too pleased either as he had to stay behind to bring both Jim and the deputy out. But such incidents brought brief moments of hilarity to our gloomy existence.

It soon became obvious that most men wore clogs rather than boots. But these were no ordinary clogs. To be really 'in' you had to make your own. This was not as difficult as it may sound.

At a local clogger's you could buy a pair of clog soles for about two bob – ten pence in modern money – and a set of irons, including a pair of smaller inner irons which fitted in the centre of the sole, not usually necessary for the clogs worn in applications other than mining. These inner irons not only protected the wood of the sole, but were extremely useful to trammers who could then slide along the tram rails with one foot on each rail on a down grade or when they wanted to apply a braking force to their moving tubs, as the inner irons fitted neatly on the rails.

Living in an area where mining blended with textiles, everybody knew somebody who worked 'at t' mill' and so there was usually a supply of used carding leather. This had a corrugated surface and was used on rollers for drawing woollen yarn from one part of a process to another, the purpose of which I have never had any inclination to find out. However, the corrugations did give a stylish appearance to the finished article of footwear. All that was necessary was to cut out four pieces, two for each clog, one to go round the fore part of the clog and the other to go round the back encasing the heel. It meant experimenting with brown paper to establish suitable templates for these shapes but once made and kept, you could make your own individual clogs forever. The top surface of the wood soles were shaped to accommodate the foot and there was a rebate all round into which the leather was fitted, then held in place with a length of copper strip and nails. When new, the copper strip added a dashing appearance but this did not last long. The final decision was whether to use laces and holes or clips to fasten the clogs on your feet. Clips were best, because they did not take much fastening when you had to get ready for work in the middle of the night, and they did not rely on knots which never remained tied.

Clogs had many advantages over boots for us. They had a solid unbending sole which you could get against the sleepers of the track and thus give a stronger push without bending the foot, particularly when pushing up hill. They kept your feet warmer in winter, particularly in snow as there was nearly an inch of wood between the sole of your foot and the ground. A significant advantage was their ability to self-customise to your feet. What happened was that they tended to fill with the coal dust and ground-up stone dust which abounded underground and with the sweat from your feet this soon formed a sort of concrete which adapted to the unique shape of your own foot and so became very comfortable.

It was a little while after I had become used to walking down the lane in all the glory of my working clothes and in my unwashed condition, that one fine afternoon I met the lady who was the proprietress of our local fish and chip shop. She was walking towards me.

During the days of wartime when local newspapers were severely restricted by the supply of printing paper and most of the younger staff had been recruited to the forces, they could not report adequately everything that occurred. At such times it fell to such worthy ladies as our fish shop proprietress to gather news and circulate it in the neighbourhood, which she did with more than adequate enthusiasm from behind her counter.

Our closing speed was not particularly great and I was a little disconcerted by the look of suspicion and apprehension with which she regarded me. When we were within speaking distance I offered a polite and appropriate greeting. The poor woman visibly flinched, turned her head away and ignored my friendly approach with contemptuous disdain. I did not think too much about it.

A few nights later my mother went to the fish shop for our traditional West Riding supper. My mother, of course, had to wait in the small queue which always formed because in those days few fish and chip shops had really mastered the technique of having an adequate supply of both fish and chips ready to be served at the same time. Either the fish would be sizzling invitingly away with no chips, or the chips would be curling up as they waited for the fish to achieve the desirable succulent quality which marked the West Riding fish and chips. The next time the fish and chip lady saw my mother in the shop she began to hold forth. In dramatic terms she told how she had been walking up the lane minding her own business – a rare occurrence – when she had been accosted by a dirty, disreputable looking tramp. She did not know whether to scream for the police or just run.

'Do you know?' she asked her eager audience of customers before looking at my mother. 'It were t' missis's son! He is one of them there Bevin Boys! Eeeeeh, it must be horrible for you Missis!'

My mother was not overcome by flattery, and despite her ability to brush this remark off it was some time before she really came to terms with it.

There were few real joys given to those who toiled underground for coal, but one of the rare ones was to emerge from the infernal darkness of the mine into a fine warm summer's day as a golden sun shone overhead from a fleecy cloud-bedecked firmament. It was on such an afternoon that Alf and I were on our way home. We had got off the bus and were walking along the road which eventually led to our homes. It was mid-afternoon and the merry clatter of our clogs reverberated from the rows of stone-built terrace cottages and factory walls that lined our route. Alf and I were good friends, we did not need to talk much; the sound of our clogs provided sufficient accompaniment to our weary thoughts as we enjoyed the sunshine. It was unlikely that we were to suffer from sunburn through the grime which encased our countenances.

About half way along Rook Lane, for such was the name of the road we followed, there was the back end of a single-storey weaving shed. Occupying the walls of the shed which abutted on to the pavement were some poster hoardings with posters newly pasted on. The men who had stuck the posters to the hoardings were nowhere to be seen; presumably they were taking their afternoon break. On the parapet of the roof of the weaving shed there were a number of mill lads and lasses who had sneaked out of the back door of the mill during their tea-break and had taken advantage of the bill posters' ladders to enjoy the sunshine on the roof of the shed.

Roused by the cheerful sound of our clogs they all looked in our direction as we approached. Some of the boys, feeling safe and superior from their vantage point, began to hurl epithets of abuse in our direction.

They made particular reference to the colour of our skins, casting doubts on our parentage and used words that even in those days the lowest would not repeat in the presence of women, not even if they were mill girls. As I may have mentioned before, Alf was gifted with lightning-quick thought which I could only admire and envy. Turning his head slightly and looking at me through the corners of his eyes, he said, 'Quick, the ladder!' I knew exactly what to do. As one man we ran across the road, seized the ladder which had given our sunbathing textile workers access to the roof, ran round the corner into another street and hurled the ladder over a wall on to some common land. We then returned to Rook Lane and waved cheerily to the workers who were stuck on the roof. Perhaps our prank was unfair on the bill posters, perhaps they should not have deserted their post, but we never had to suffer jibes and insults from those mill workers again.

A further incident was to demonstrate that our appearance did not only cause derision but sometimes abject terror. On another occasion Alf and I were on our way home. We were walking along, only a few doors away from the house where Alf lived. As we got nearer we saw two schoolboys, of about eight or nine years old coming along the street ringing doorbells and running away before the occupant could get to the door. Oddly they had not noticed us because when the senior of the two rang Alf's doorbell he had no idea we were there. As the child came running towards us from Alf's front garden gate, Alf blocked his way. He did not touch the boy, but just asked, 'Now then what do you think you are doing?'

The effect was astonishing and completely unexpected by both Alf and myself. The poor child stopped in his tracks raised his eyes to our blackened faces and was overcome by extreme terror. We suddenly found ourselves standing in a rapidly expanding pool of water which appeared to emanate from the area of the unfortunate youthful mischiefmaker. Alf burst out laughing, and knowing where the child lived took him home to explain to his mother what had happened and to recommend a change of underwear for the unhappy miscreant. This incident brought about an end to the scourge of the phantom doorbell ringers in the area.

Another of our miners, keen on maintaining his sartorial elegance, had gone for an afternoon and night out with some of his colleagues to the local Big City. While there they had, for some reason, visited a local exhibition of waxworks, doubtless in the quest to improve their education and to broaden their minds. One of the effigies was a replica of Charles Peace, the villainous Victorian felon – he gets a mention in the Sherlock Holmes story, *The Illustrious Client* – but this member of the party took a fancy to the flat cap that Charlie Peace was wearing and thought its appearance too bright and new to be appropriate to the malefactor. He was quick to discover that the cap was the same size as his own. It was but the work of a few seconds to effect an exchange and his colleagues were impressed not only by this example of quick thinking, but the enhanced appearance of Charles Peace and the look of elegance attained by their opportunity-seizing colleague.

There was one collier there whom I shall never forget – Fred Larthorpe. Fred was a keen gardener, as indeed many were. He lived in a small neat cottage – not far from the pit – and his small front garden was always a joy to behold. The choice of his plants, and the blend of colours made many stop and stare. He also had an allotment. I soon found that Fred was the soul of generosity. If you were tramming for Fred and he thought you had put your back into it for him, there would be a handsome tip in your pay packet, particularly before a bank holiday. The pay structure was rather odd, or different to the usual industrial organisation. Our pay as Bevin Boys was in two parts: the colliers we worked for paid a certain amount and the colliery management paid the rest to make it up to the decreed minimum, which was £5 per week at twenty-one. So I was quite surprised when I received my first tip from Fred one Easter. There were not many who did recognise our efforts although perhaps they had enough on to eke out a living themselves.

Fred was a friendly soul and once we were talking about gardening, a subject about which I knew nothing. Fred did the talking and I would say 'Yes' or 'No' in what I thought were the right places. Eventually he asked me what were my favourite flowers. All I could think of was Sweet Williams, and this was only because at school we had a teacher whom we all called Sweet William. I thought little more of this conversation but the following morning Fred was waiting for me at the lamp room. He had a large bouquet of Sweet Williams which he gave to me. They were carefully wrapped in newspaper so they would not get dusty or damaged during their day down the pit. When I took them home my mother could not believe they had survived a shift underground.

Fred was what I think they call 'one of nature's Gentlemen'. We never heard him swear and always he set the standard for the well-dressed collier. Every day during the appropriate season he came to work sporting a floral buttonhole in his pit clothes – usually a carnation when available, but new every day. Fred, bless him was a man with natural dignity. I still like to have Sweet Williams growing in our garden, but I do not need a memento to remind me of Fred.

The prop setter
Impression by Jane Flower

Pillars of the Community

To nearly everybody, one of the greatest joys in this mortal vale of tears is the food we eat and those of us condemned to a subterranean existence, were no exception. Apart from the time to have a break, technically for twenty minutes, the appetite engendered by heavy toil encouraged you to look forward to your snap, or bait. Understandably in wartime there could be few epicurean delights granted to us but we did enjoy what we could get. Now, sixty years afterwards, my menu may seem bizarre to today's healthy eaters. For myself I liked to take cheese sandwiches, particularly with fresh onion, but I enjoyed eating the onion as an accompaniment, eating it like an apple rather than sliced up in the sandwich. An alternative was cheese and treacle, preferably dark treacle – something I would only contemplate now in an attempt to revive old memories and desires.

Perhaps the work made demands on the digestive system and gave us tastes that would rarely be thought of by people who lived normal lives on the surface. I always enjoyed a sticky malt loaf, all at one go. Peanut butter sandwiches were at first eagerly anticipated, but it was amazing how soon the enthusiasm for these delicacies palled and the thought of peanut butter, even now, fires me with little enthusiasm. The universal drink was cold tea; it really is the only drink that slakes a thirst. I liked it without sugar or milk. This way it was sufficiently bitter to discourage drinking all at once.

However it did require some discipline to avoid drinking your supply all at once, as it was essential to leave enough to swill your mouth out at the end of the shift. Occasionally it was possible to get Lemon Barley crystals and these made a drink which was a refreshing change, but again by the time you had used the entire packet you had had enough and welcomed the return to tea.

While we were supposed to have but twenty minutes for our break, we could usually extend this by a few minutes, either until the colliers shouted that they wanted their coal moving, or when we recognised the distinctive glow from the deputy's light heralding his approach. If he caught us he would chivvy us up and encourage us to get back to work with threats of appearances before the production committee. But there was one by-worker, Jimmy Metcalfe, and to be assigned to Jimmy was a stroke of luck. A long break was guaranteed if you played your cards right even though he was a conscientious hard working man. Jimmy owned a Morris 8 open tourer. Obviously it was a pre-war model, but he had looked after it and kept it in tip-top condition. He was allowed a small ration of fuel to come to work in it. But by careful and prudent use he was able to save some of his ration for his main passion in life, trips to the glorious Yorkshire Dales.

If, for instance, you had come to the end of the snap-break and Jimmy would be picking up his tools to start work again, a simple question was all that was needed. 'Jimmy, have you ever seen the ebbing and flowing well at Giggleswick Scar and have you ever seen it actually ebbing and flowing?'

It should be explained that this phenomenon was one of many in the limestone area of North West Yorkshire. This was a stone horsetrough at the side of the road up Giggleswick Scar to Buckhaw Brow on the way to Morecambe. It was unusual in that the water in the trough would rise and fall like a mini-tidal system. Such a question would stop Jimmy in his tracks. He would put his pick or shovel down and contemplate the distance with a wistful look.

He would think a bit, then, 'Yes,' he had seen this intriguing well in action and not only that, his father who had first taken him to see it had actually seen the Silver Thread – an amazing effect caused by a string of bubbles which would occasionally manifest itself as the well went into action. This Silver Thread was expected to bring good luck to the beholder, but so far it had brought no signs of good fortune to Jimmy's dad.

If you were stopping work to 'have a minute' – an essential short rest to get your breath back – it would be a good time to ask another Dales-related question. Is it really fatal to fall into the Strid in Bolton Abbey Woods? This is where the turbulent river Wharfe flows through a narrow chasm in the rock about five-feet wide. Jimmy would stop to think of happier places and answer your question in full. Was Hardraw Force, near Hawes, really the longest single waterfall in England? This would always precipitate a good long discussion. Despite these interruptions he always managed to get through his appointed work, and it was always more entertaining and instructive than the routine of a regular day.

At the end of the shift we wandered to the canteen, where a motherly sort of lady provided remarkable meals considering that it was wartime. There was always something which was both filling and appetising and, of course, pit canteen tea. I don't know what the secret of this tea was but they still make it at mining museums.

After lingering over our pots of tea, we would then saunter across the road to the bus stop to wait for our homeward transport. An ordinary service bus was the normal conveyance, which would be already half filled with 'civilians' by the time it got to our stop.

We filled it up. Then we found that many of the civilians were not always very civil. They did not like dirty miners sitting next to them, even though we were more likely than not wearing overcoats or raincoats which covered our working clothes. Eventually the normal passengers complained to the bus company about we pillars of the community, engaged in essential war work, and a special bus was put on. Even though it started from the pit, and was marked 'special' it was often half full by the time we got on board.

When waiting for the bus, if it was a fine afternoon we would sit on the causeway edge and discuss the traffic, world affairs, lateness of buses, and so on. One day as we sat there in a neat row, waiting patiently for our bus to arrive, there was a sudden rush of excitement. Two police motorcyclists materialised leading a cavalcade of dignified Daimlers. These cars must have been old when our parents were young. They were tall and high, and whoever rode in them could enter them without bending. There was a considerable contrast between the dress and appearance of those who rode in them and our merry tribe.

Nobody said much as the cars went past apart from making

facetious comments about the likelihood of owning such a vehicle on a miner's pay.

A few days later a letter appeared on the notice-board outside the pay office from 'Her Royal Highness's secretary'. It expressed disappointment that the men employed at the colliery had remained seated in the gutter and had not stood up as Her Royal Highness's car had gone past. Our manager made no comment, but thought we would love to see the letter.

He was well able to deflect the flood of requests from his work-force that we should be supplied with bowler hats and pin-stripe trousers in case the situation should repeat itself.

Alf and I became friendly with one of the coal-lorry drivers who came on a fairly regular basis to collect loads of coal for distribution to various mills and factories. In a small way he helped to solve our transport problem. His route took him past the road end where we lived and he would willingly give us a lift. He said he always liked talking to us. What we accepted as a life of monotonous toil sounded to him like a life of adventure. Perhaps it was the way we told our stories.

His vehicle was a big Leyland Titan or Tiger or something like that. The bonnet stuck out in front of the driving cab, so there was plenty of room inside. There was a great big gear lever, and when changing gear – often by the mysterious process of double-de-clutching – the vehicle would appear to go for miles during the process. 'I have time to go to the loo when changing gear,' he told us reassuringly. On fine summer days he would let us sit on top of the load of coal he carried.

This was always a refreshingly invigorating never-to-be forgotten experience. It always gave us a thrill of importance as we climbed down to the pavement at the end of our journey a bit like rich holidaymakers disembarking from a luxury cruise, but not as well dressed, when watched by envious passers-by.

Another pillar of the community was our bus driver, a man whose sense of purpose and determination went far above and beyond the call of duty. We never discovered his name. Every morning, regardless of weather conditions, his bus turned up at our stop promptly at 6.15 a.m.

During the heavy snows of early 1947, there had been yet

another heavy snowfall during the night, which had been whipped up into a frenzied blizzard by strong winds. Alf and I had decided that we must make an effort to get to work, not for any reasons of patriotic fervour but because we already had used up our limit of unofficial days off for that month, and any more would have put us in front of the dreaded production committee, unless we had a legitimate excuse – such as the bus not turning up because of the weather. We huddled together sat on the low shop window at the bus stop and our hearts sank when we saw the bus materialising out of the snow-laden darkness. The bus was a double-decker, with an outside staircase at the back open to the elements. What made it go was a big Gardiner diesel engine which projected a foot further out from the front than the original supplied by the makers. It also had a plaque on the side to say that it had been sent to help out London Transport during the blitz and that it had survived this exemplary war service to return to its own ground.

It had a heater in the downstairs saloon but all it did was to make a whirring sound which encouraged the passengers to get as near to it as possible. Nobody ever admitted to detecting any warmth from it. It was so cold on this morning that even the conductress huddled together with us passengers in a feeble attempt to get warm.

Our sturdy vehicle moaned and groaned as the driver wrestled with the wheel to maintain his course through the raging elements. At last he had to stop. We all looked out through the snow-encrusted windows and our spirits rose when we saw an enormous snow drift about fifteen feet high crossing the road at about forty-five degrees. It had been formed by the gale blowing between two house ends.

It now became evident that the driver had no alternative but to turn his bus round, abandon his journey and take us back home. But no. He was made of sterner stuff, the stuff of which heroes were made. He climbed down from his cab and examined the fluting curves of sculpted snow which resembled something from a photograph that Herbert Ponting or Frank Hurley might have taken not much more than thirty years previously in the Antarctic. The driver came to the conclusion that at one end the drift was much thinner than the other and that there might just be enough room to force his vehicle through. We pleaded with him. We reminded him that he should endanger neither his vehicle nor the lives of his crew and passengers. But to no avail. The nation was not to be deprived of its coal because of any lack of moral fibre on the part of bus drivers. He gave us the choice – we could get out and watch or stay where we were and give the vehicle some extra ballast.

We chose to stay where it was relatively warm, at least more protected from the elements than standing outside. The conductress got out and helped to guide the bus though the icy chasm. So with a lot of grinding noises and mighty shudderings the vehicle emerged at the other side of the drift, much to our disappointment. Few believed the story of the unchecked heroism of our humble driver, still less when the time came to make the return journey and the snow ploughs had removed all trace of our almost impassable impasse.

Alf and I also did our bit for the community in a modest sort of way. Walking home we usually passed a row of terraced cottages, of the back-to-back, one-up and one-down variety. One afternoon, a housewife was standing at one of the doors, which opened directly on to the pavement with no front garden.

She asked us if it was our clogs she could hear at 6 a.m. every morning. At first we thought she was going to complain, but no, what she wanted was the services of a knocker-upper, someone to bang on the door every morning at 6 a.m. I had always been intrigued by stories of professional knockers-up. It was well-known that a highly skilled practitioner of the craft could awaken the middle person of three sharing a bed, and I was willing to attempt a new skill.

The reward was to be sixpence (old money) per week to be shared. I asked if it would not be a shrewder investment to buy an alarm clock, but no, that required too extravagant an outlay. It was evident that this lady came from prudent, careful stock unlikely to make rash financial decisions.

One of the conditions was that we should knock until a bedroom light came on. We readily accepted; this was easy money. It was not explained that they did not need to be awoken from their slumbers on Saturday mornings. In any case we were always half an hour earlier on Saturdays. We were to be paid on Friday afternoons as we made our way home.

We collected our first sixpence but could not remember as we walked past on the Saturday morning if they wanted to be awoken. Alf decided that they had as much right to be awake at that time as we had and accomplished the task with enthusiasm. We collected three sixpences and were told each time that we were paid not to wake them up on Saturdays. After the fourth Saturday we approached the house eager to accept our sixpence only to be greeted with a bitter disappointment. The house was empty.

There were no curtains in the window, nothing but a sign 'HOUSE TO LET' and the scratched door panel where our clogs had performed such sterling work.

Had our knocking-up service been too enthusiastic? Had we driven these humble dwellers from their cosy roadside home? We never found the answer to that and for over fifty years I have had this on my conscience. We never got paid for our fourth week; such is man's and woman's ingratitude.

Enterprise, Fear and a Touch of Envy

During the long hours of darkness – a phrase usually associated with winter nights – but here the long hours spent in the underground darkness, you would think of what you could be doing on the surface, or what you should be doing on the surface to *addle some brass*. This was a mid-Yorkshire expression which meant to earn some money.

But there was not a lot that you could do in wartime; in any case most of us were much too tired to even think about it. Ernest Holdsworth lived but a few hundred yards from the pit-head. He lived in a ground floor flat in an odd sort of building. The first floor had a meeting room where Madame Zelda taught ballroom dancing. The building stood in a small paddock where a horse and donkey roamed freely between the hawthorn hedge and the trees which marked the boundary of the property.

Ernest would amble home at the end of his shift and flop into an old comfortable rocking chair and then succumb to a deep slumber. Most of us did this when we got home in some way or other. Ernest lived by himself; there was no soft female touch to ease his hardy existence. 'What is home without a mother?' was the taunt that fell from everybody's lips. Some would even say his was 'a face that only a mother could love'. Ernest took it all in good part. However, one sunny summer afternoon he had pulled his rocking chair close to his open front door where he could relax in the warming rays of the afternoon sun and soon fell hard and fast asleep.

He was awakened by a relatively rare occurrence. He was recipient of a warm wet kiss. Slowly he recovered from his deep slumber, relishing every tender touch which caressed his unshaven cheek. Swiftly he awoke to the horror of his situation. There was no lissom lovely from the dancing academy lavishing love and affection. From the paddock was the humble donkey which had idly ventured through the open door and had started to lick Ernest's coal-dust encrusted face. It may be that the donkey had worshipped Ernest from afar for some time, but more likely that it found the mixture of salt, sweat and coal dust which encased Ernest's visage, 'the face that only a mother could love', completely irresistible.

He encouraged the donkey to leave his sparse living room and tried to return to his sleep, but this, of course, was now impossible. Fortunately the lowly beast of burden left no trace of its visit. Next day Ernest took great delight in describing the embarrassment of having a donkey in his home with much enthusiasm. Doubtless the adventure gained a little every time it was told. This was not a world shattering adventure but Ernest got much mileage from it.

Another collier, or proper miner – we Bevin Boys were never really regarded as proper miners – found the need to augment his meagre income as Christmas approached. From somewhere he acquired some moulds to make model soldiers. This was during a time of shortages and toys were scarce. The material required was lead, also in short supply, but our model manufacturer found this no serious impediment to his business project.

Not too far away was a steadily decaying terrace of derelict cottages, the type of one-up and one-downers that had been lit by gas. Each had but one water tap. Here was a ready supply of lead piping – the danger of lead piping was not appreciated in those days – and so our entrepreneur, already well-equipped with instinctive mining techniques, was soon in a position to extract the material for his miniature warriors. Choosing a time of darkness – it was already dark early in the evening – our would-be toy producer began his furtive task. He was not aware that the water had not been turned off. The resulting flooded properties initiated inquiries by the locals and eventually the missing owner was found. Because the prospective toy producer was of previous good character, he was bound over to keep the peace, a penalty which did not entitle him to retain ownership of his raw material, and unhappily brought to an end his well-intended attempts to brighten the lives of local children.

The need for self-expression and the urge to demonstrate skill in the graphic arts can bring to the surface surprising ingenuity in unexpected situations. At the time when there was an outbreak of potato blight, or some other such devastating disease threatening to eradicate the humble root vegetable, there came about a release of artistic talent in a most unexpected individual, one who had shown little interest in the arts. This was Maurice Barford whose fertile creative talent was kindled by an official poster he saw opposite his bus stop offering a generous reward for the capture of Colorado beetles. He read the description and closely examined the illustration which was there to aid identification of the insects thought to be responsible for the blight. The beetles did not look a great deal different from the common ladybird.

The Colorado beetle had yellow and black stripes along its wing cases, instead of the familiar black dots on a red ground as sported by the common ladybird. Maurice borrowed his young sister's paintbox and a fine paint brush. He caught a few ladybirds in the local allotments. At first he found it difficult getting the ladybirds to keep still. But eventually by means of a few deft strokes of the paint brush, he had some very passable Colorado beetles. He submitted them to the appropriate authority, only to get his first rejection slip with an acid comment on his brushwork technique and a suggestion that he may have taken part in an activity which was not strictly legal. It was a brave attempt to make a bob or two on the side. Thinking about it in retrospect, if Maurice had mounted a few of his Colorados in random fashion on a sheet of plastic, he would probably have been the darling of the avant-garde art experts of today.

Yet another miner came to work one Monday morning, his face as long as a fiddle. He had been done, he told us all, almost with a hint of pride that there was somebody who could actually pull a fast one over him. For some time he had been troubled with cockroaches and had sought all means of getting rid of them. Every Saturday there was a market at his local town and there he had bought a kit which was to solve his problem. The kit for killing cockroaches which cost him half-a-crown, explained that the system was one hundred percent effective. Full instructions were included. When he got home and opened the box he found two small blocks of wood marked A and B. The instructions were as concise as they were simple. 'PLACE THE COCKROACH

ON BLOCK "A" AND STRIKE SMARTLY WITH BLOCK "B".'

We each felt that here was a warning for us all. There was yet another evil insect which occasionally appeared underground, one which not only inspired downright loathing but sometimes panic and intense fear.

This dreaded insect was the saw-fly. I never bothered to find out what its generic name was and I did not see many of these creatures, although I did hear them. It was something like a largish wasp and in flight it made a noise a bit like a miniature helicopter and if one flew into you in the dark you were invariably overcome with a feeling of intense revulsion and loathing. Perhaps if it had been possible to see them they may not have felt so horrible. It appeared that they came in infected wood (pit-props) and hatched out underground. The danger they caused was that they drilled into the pit-props to provide a place for their eggs to hatch, consequently weakening the props and resulting in possible roof collapse. I had never heard of this actually happening but some of the miners took their presence very seriously. One man broke a shovel when he tried to kill a saw-fly that he saw on a tub rail, such was the force of his strike.

Of course there were apocryphal stories about the saw-flies. One was that our manager had come into the district to investigate what he thought were hysterical reports of the presence of these creatures. He demanded that someone should produce an example of this detested creature, but nobody had either caught or killed one. When shown the bore holes in the props he dismissed them as something that had happened on the surface and that the complainants should grow up and not be so superstitious.

While conducting this harangue he began scratching the back of his neck with an air of nonchalance. Suddenly his body went rigid; the back of his helmet hit the roof, as he pulled the mangled corpse of one of these insects out of the back of his shirt neck. It looked as if the creature had mistaken the back of his neck for a pit-prop and had begun to bore. Some of the miners said afterwards that this would have been more understandable had the fly mistaken the manager's head for a wooden pit-prop.

I suppose the saw-flies were something like the Great Wood Horntail, one of the many wasps which afflict our shores. If they inspired some kind of fear it was of a temporary, passing nature, not entirely like the continuous nagging subconscious fear that was a permanent feature of underground life, especially to those not born to a subterranean life-style. From the thrill of apprehension at the first descent into the bowels of the underworld at the training colliery, right until eventually gaining complete freedom from the pit, there was never any escape from the thoughts of what might happen. But this was wartime and one could not forget either, the horrors which others in the armed forces would have to face on a daily basis, but particularly those in the other great civilian front line service, the Merchant Navy.

There was some comfort in the thought that no one was deliberately trying to kill us. The possibility of well-aimed enemy bombs hitting the downcast and upcast shafts was quite remote but not beyond the bounds of possibility.

I was fortunate that no serious accidents occurred when I was working. On the whole I came to accept underground existence. I always took a last look at what we could see of the sky every time we went down, regardless of whether it was darkness or daylight. It was always great to see daylight at the end of each shift. And what a joy it was to catch a glimpse of the nearby Hawthorne tree, bright and green in the springtime as the cage came to the top. A sprig of Hawthorne was always good to chew after the end of a shift. It was supposed to taste of bread and cheese, but it was always refreshing and was a traditional mark of the miner in those days.

At the training colliery we had been warned of the phenomenon of 'the weight coming on'. This was presumably to prevent panic attacks if ever we should experience this fearsome happening. This happened when mother earth eventually wanted to settle down a bit after layers of coal had been removed. No amount of props or packing the gob with waste stone could prevent earth's display of displeasure. This would usually manifest itself by a sound very much like thunder, with dust and small fragments falling from the roof to the accompaniment of groaning pit-props.

This could be very alarming the first time you experienced it and no less so, the second. Our manager had warned us not to worry. If the worst possibility happened and the space where the coal-seam had been closed up entirely we would still be able to crawl out, because the gates and crossgates, and so on, were usually four to five feet high, and as the seam was only twenty-two to twenty-four inches high there would be space left for us to find our way out, but thank God it never came to that extremity.

Down our pit, which I do not suppose was unique, there were what were known as potholes. These occurred in the roof. These were not holes in the ground to be explored by the adventurous, but usually bell-shaped disturbances in the even strata of the coal-bearing stone. These were separated from the rest of the rock by a thin layer of coal about a quarter inch thick. If they were not recognised and held in place with props and bar legs, and so on, they could suddenly fall out of the roof with disastrous results to anybody underneath. It is surprising how quickly the mind can work in a situation where the subconscious never forgets the ambient dangers. Only a small fragment of stone had to drop on to your back or the back of the helmet and you were reminded that you were not immortal.

I was lucky in that I was never involved in a serious accident, which were comparatively rare. I did once find myself in a roof fall. This was when I was working with Norman, a man known for his unwillingness to engage in idle chatter – he just wanted to get on with the work. In the twenty-two inch seam where the regulations required that no prop should be more than two feet from the face or from another prop, the working space was limited. It was an easy temptation to bend the rules and not observe the letter of the law strictly. Whether Norman had been tempted I do not know, but there was a sudden creaking of wood, a rumbling, and then a great big slab of stone with lots of debris fell from the roof. The roof was only the height of the thickness of the seam, but the pile of rubble left me no means of escape to the next face to get help. Although un-injured, thoughts of escape were erased by the need to find out what had happened to Norman.

He was stuck, trapped by his legs. The other side of the slab was pinning him across his thighs, with a nasty gash to the bone.

I could not get out. I shouted at the top of my voice hoping someone would hear. I had to try to do something about the horrible wound in Norman's leg. What could I do? This was a gaping wound, with no means of keeping it clean in the filthy dust-laden atmosphere with little room to move about. I tried to hold the wound together and tried to slow the flow of blood.

It was surprising how quickly help came, how everybody worked together to get Norman out and away for proper medical attention. The deputy turned up and after Norman had been made comfortable and sent to the pit bottom, the deputy asked if I was all right. I was okay. So I should get back to work as there was now a glut of tubs in the crossgate all wanting to be shifted.

The next day Norman was back at work. He had to be, he needed the money. They had sewn up his wound and bound it well with bandages. If he was careful his stitches would hold. I was not the only one to be shocked but when we asked the older miners, all we could get was, 'He needs the money.' Norman recovered without breaking time, but his continued work was not inspired by the nation's need for coal. He needed the money.

This was the nearest that I came to being in a pit accident and I don't remember being unduly overwhelmed by the panic which I expected would automatically follow such an incident. No work meant no pay, and Norman needed the money. For myself the near prospect of being buried alive left me just a little bit shaken. It was a bit like the first time you fall off your motorbike. If you don't get back on and drive again, you never will. I got back to work and never told anybody at home about my adventure.

Some of the neighbours were not always ready to acknowledge me as I walked home in my working gear but with experience I did not get as dirty. Our house was a small semi with only one fire place and a fireback boiler to heat the water. All the houses in the row were like this. In all probability, if cleanliness was next to godliness I should have been the most reverend dweller in the row. In those days few people had a bath every day, as I did, and central heating was unheard of. It was difficult enough keeping the house warm on the ration of coal allowed – five bags a month. During the long hard winter of 1947, the coal delivery could not be relied upon to arrive on time. The threat of being without coal when the snow was knee-deep outside and the water pipes only too willing to freeze up, was a real one.

We Bevin Boys at our colliery were not classed as proper miners and so were not entitled to 'home coal' which was about the only perk that the real miners got. But as a concession we were allowed a load, that is, a ton of coal once a month at pit-head prices, which represented a saving. This was probably due to us having no pit-head baths. But back to the winter of 1947, and a time when the snow had been really bad and our lane was virtually impassable. Modern newspapers today would say it was blocked. Everybody in the row was running out of their meagre coal allowance fast and there was no sign of any delivery. Our own coal-house was almost empty and I was almost faced with the possibility of having to get bathed in water boiled in the kettle.

One day as I plodged home through the snow I was pleased to see the Co-op coal man delivering our monthly ration. With his horse and cart he had managed to get through where motor transport failed.

My cup really began to overflow when another horse-drawn coal cart arrived on the scene shortly afterwards with a ton of glistening, shining black diamonds which were dumped at our front gate for all the world to see.

My popularity soared. People who had not spoken to me for a couple of years would compliment me on my work of national importance, and was there any chance of a bucket of coal? There was still a fuel shortage for some time after the war – it was an unhappy situation. The friendly neighbours who had always been sympathetic, never even hinted to me at their own shortage of coal.

The only time that we looked forward to getting down the pit with something approaching enthusiasm was during this same long winter of 1947. We were always able to get to work, the main road was kept open, and the large brazier burning at the mouth of the downcast shaft was a cheerful, welcoming sight. This was kept going day and night during the coldest weather to warm up the air being sucked into the pit to prevent ice forming on the walls of the shaft. Most would stand near the fire to get warmed up after the journey to the colliery. But rarely did they linger for a warm-up on their way home.

On the Move

The time was passing irrevocably and slowly, the only changes being the procession of the seasons. Autumn would give way to winter. It was not the cold that was so daunting as much as the thought that, like the production workers at the aircraft factory, we would only be seeing daylight on Sunday. Until the end of the war it was a six-day week that we worked, although Saturday was a shorter day – we started half-an-hour earlier but finished ninety minutes earlier. What a relief it was to be eventually put on a five-day week. None of us ever knew when or how we would be released, or demobbed as it would have been in the forces. There was much discussion, many questions and many suggestions. Quite a few wanted to have their notification of release framed to hang on the sitting-room wall, where it would become the focus of attention when 'respectable' people came for Sunday afternoon tea.

But this was a long way in the future. It was on 6 June 1945, that the war in Europe came to an end. This vital news came to us chalked on the side of a tub half-way through a shift. 'War Over' the simple message said. We did not believe it. Was it some prankster at the pit-head? But we could not think of any one who was capable of such a jest. Eventually the deputy got a message through on his telephone confirming the momentous news. Did this mean we could all run to the pit bottom and escape from our unwanted calling forever?

Our deputy could understand our joy but was insistent that we stayed at work, which we did for a long time after VE Day and even after VJ Day, the day the war ended with Japan.

Life dropped back into its regular pattern, but with a little more leeway now that Saturday was free. Now it was possible to spend weekends out walking in the countryside, the Yorkshire Dales – hiking is a word that has always made me shudder – staying at the YHA properties which were reasonably plentiful and which could be reached using public transport, although with a bit of a tidy effort. There were arguments with others who preferred to go cycling, but living on top of a hill there was no way to get home without peddling up a long incline. Occasionally I would meet up with a group of lads from one of the larger south Yorkshire pits. I was always impressed by their system of communicating their arrangements to one another when working different shifts in different districts. They would chalk their time and meeting place on one of the main ventilation doors near the pit bottom where the messages could be seen by all.

I had a group of friends whom I had known since my remote Sunday school days. They would invite me to join them in a game of tennis during the summer months, a genteel game regarded with suspicion and as something a little bit socially unacceptable by my workmates. I cannot call to mind the picturesque phrases they used to describe this game at which I was useless in any case.

My respectable, but well-meaning surface friends suggested I should go to Saturday night dances with them.

It was a mixed group and in those days – before sex was invented – the dance-hall was a good place to meet new girls. At the interval there would be tea, lemonade, sandwiches and pork pies, and so on for the well-behaved.

Those who were already familiar with the demon drink could renew their acquaintance by getting a pass-out which enabled them to leave the dance-hall and get back in again without having to pay for re-entry. The dance-hall we went to was one of two which shared the same roof. These were known as King's and Queen's Halls. The King's Hall was in fact the city swimming baths. In winter a temporary floor covered the bath itself and you could go and watch all-in wrestling as it was then known, a popular mid-Pennine spectator entertainment which might have lost some of its cosy intimacy with the advent of TV. A ring was put up in the middle of the floor and the raised seats which lined the bath were an ideal place for the enthusiasts to sit. Those who sat at the ends and were the greater distance from the action paid less than those who sat directly opposite the ring.

The Queen's Hall was infinitely superior to the King's; for a start it had a proper sprung dance floor and upholstered seating accommodation round the floor and on the semicircular balcony which overlooked the dance floor. Tasteful classical statues were arranged in various alcoves to give a reassuring feeling of class. The entire building was built on a slope and so the Queen's as it was known, was not only superior in height but also in the class and quality of person to be encountered there.

If it was 1/9d to get in the King's, it was 2/6d to get in the Queen's. The floor of the Queen's was about five feet above the floor of the King's. The two were separated by a raised stage, and a safety curtain could be lowered to separate the two completely, as indeed it was when the King's was used for swimming.

The siting of the band – oh yes, it was live music, not tinned – was a stroke of West Riding economic genius. The musicians sat on the stage more or less facing each other with the bandleader or soloists in the centre. In this way both dance-halls had the advantage of just one band. If there was any bias or favouritism displayed by the band, this would be directed to the more exclusive Queen's and the patrons who wished to lavish luxury and romance on their fortunate girl-friends.

After the dance, in those puritanical days, it was usual to walk the young lady home, treating her in true romantic fashion by buying her fish and chips to eat in the street. When reaching her doorstep there would be the hope of a promise to meet again, usually a futile hope when the vision of loveliness discovered that by day you worked down the pit. National service was not a good fashionable excuse.

Then it was back to work on Monday mornings. The tyrannical ring of the alarm clock brought the amazingly short night to an end and back to getting ready for work, dressing in dirty working clothes. There were no pit-head baths or lockers where working gear could be kept. But once in the working gear it was easy to return to your other self, forgetting the dapper *alter ego* you were at weekends.

Once at work on a Monday morning the inevitable conversations were about what you had been doing at the weekend. It was rare that a remark would be made directly imputing, or questioning your personal love life, even though this was always a topic of universal interest.

Nevertheless a picture of a scantily clad bathing beauty, as they were known in those days, in the leading tabloid newspaper used to wrap up somebody's sandwiches would spark off imaginative and appreciative comments.

There was quite a stir when an attractive modern young woman was dismissed from her post as a secretary at one of the larger local textile mills. Her offence was to appear in the centrefold of a well-known national magazine which encouraged the promotion of health by abandoning clothes. None of us knew this ravishingly delightful and shapely young woman but an increasingly dog-eared copy of the magazine was passed along the coal-face and eagerly scrutinised by all and sundry needing a little light relief in their overwhelming darkness. The magazine soon sold out and became unobtainable in the area.

Back to more serious matters. We were always looking for ways to ease our work-load. We Bevin Boy trammers got down to improve the tracks along which we had to push the tubs. We took more care when laying track and would straighten out awkward joins. We also found that by putting waste stone under the sleepers it was possible to level the track and take out small dips and slopes making it easier to push the tubs along.

Our most imaginative feat was a joint effort between Alf, myself and another Bevin Boy, Ted. It was a good mile and a half walk from the pit bottom to the coal-face, much of the time bent double. But this is not necessarily a correct description. The way to avoid backache and allied problems was to keep your back as straight as possible. So eventually you learnt how to lean forward slightly and walk with bended knees.

Not only was the main road low in places, it was not a level walk either. The haulage plane, as the deputies called it, went up and down a number of inclines. With one exception, these slopes were gentle, just enough for a tub to roll by gravity. The exception was an incline locally known as the drift. It was an incline about 160 yards long where the haulage road had to negotiate a geological fault which had thrown the coal-seam up ten yards to a higher level on one side.

One day the three of us came across a damaged tub in a disused heading. It had none of its sides left, apart from one plank which we were soon able to remove. We had always envied the manager his 'flat tram' and saw in this relic a solution to our own transport problem. It was an old tub with well-worn axles so with a bit of grease it would run quite freely. It was just large enough for two of us to kneel on side by side while the third could push, or at a pinch the third could squeeze on behind the other two when gravitating down slopes. Deciding the rota of who should ride and who should push was arrived at by a simple democratic process. We gave it a trial and found that it did not take too much pushing and if we timed it right we could grab the haulage rope just like the manager did when it was moving.

There were some dangers. The haulage road was no place to be when a run of full tubs was coming out. At the bottom of the drift the pulling rope would be thrashing up against the roof as it hauled the run up the slope at the other side of the summit of the drift. If we had been on our tram when this happened, it would have splattered us all over the roof. It was not a pleasant experience being on the haulage road at all if the rope broke.

Still we went ahead and soon perfected a technique for using our tram both for going in and coming out. Our personal transport did not meet with universal approval. Many of the miners would walk between the lines on their way in and on their way out.

There were a number of sections where we could get a lively speed up and it meant that they had to jump out of the way. They resented our initiative. The first time the three of us went down the drift on our tram we had no idea how fast it was going to travel. It did not frighten us sufficiently to abandon our project altogether but it was quite hairy. The air had a large dust content which turned into an impenetrable fog at the speed we travelled. Our lamps could not pierce it. We could see the lights of miners in front as they hurriedly jumped into the refuge holes which lined the route. Their first thoughts were that there was a run-away train of tubs. Our momentum carried us a long way past the bottom of the drift and we soon found a place to hide our improvised transport near the pit bottom for our journey into work the next morning.

After some discussion on the bus home we decided that our

vehicle needed some means of applying a braking force. We did not want to gain too much antagonism from our working colleagues, neither did we want to put the fear of God up ourselves as we had done. Close examination the following day, revealed that one of the pieces of wood which formed the bottom of our tram was partly broken. This plank was at right angles to the direction of travel and could be made to impinge on one of the wheels, thus giving a form of primitive braking. As the wheels were bushed solidly onto the axles, pressure on one wheel provided two-wheel breaking. We used this form of transport for about a fortnight, during which time we were never reprimanded by any member of the management team.

One morning we went to the refuge hole where we stabled our mount and there it was... gone!

It had always been forbidden to ride in the empty tubs of the moving rope-hauled trains, but much to our surprise, a few days after our flat tram had disappeared, an announcement appeared on the pit notice-board. We were to be treated to a Paddy Mail train. The Paddy Mail train was one used to transport miners from pit bottom to coal-face and back again at the end of the shift. In larger pits they could be quite elaborate, locomotive-hauled with seats and even a roof, but our pit ran to no such concessions. We were to be allowed to ride in a run of 'empties' going in to the face and a special run of empties was put on to bring us out – two men to a tub. The driver of the train was one of the senior miners, or 'trusties' as we called them, and he sat by himself in the first tub with a high candle-power lamp which was nearly strong enough to set fire to the pit-props.

His method of communication with the haulage engine driver (main and tail) was simple. He was provided with a T-shaped wand which had a strip of bare metal along the bar of the T. The signal wires which were used to relay instructions to the main and tail engine driver were now moved from the side of the heading and ran parallel to and above the centre of the track, something similar to trolleybus wires. If the driver of the train needed to signal to the engine man he touched the signal wires with his T-shaped wand and this rang the bell at the engine man's side.

There would be a code of signals to the engine man:

something like 'Three Bells – proceed inbye slowly', 'Four Bells – full speed', but most important of all – 'One Bell – *STOP!*'

Most miners were quite ingenious and the driver of our train was no exception. In those days chewing-tobacco was sold wrapped in triangles of silver foil. Several miners chewed tobacco so there were always plenty of these silver, highly reflective triangles around.

The longest edge of the triangle would be about six inches (fifteen centimetres). Our driver would collect and fasten these triangles to various pit-props at the side of the haulage way to give him a count down for bringing the train to a halt as it neared the end of its journey.

The Paddy Mail was a welcome concession and we often wondered but never actually found out whether it was coincidence, or if our modest attempt at personal transport had provoked the idea for the train. Something I will never know.

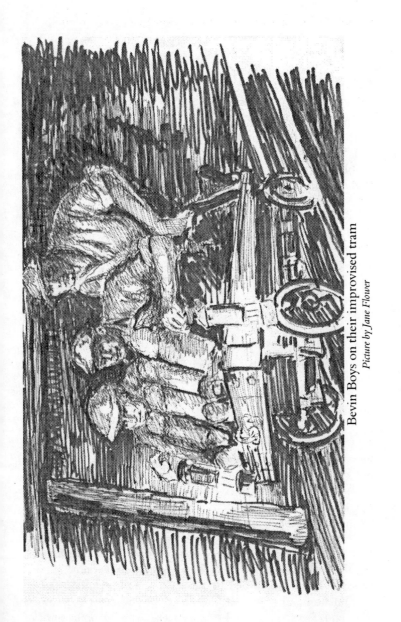

Bevin Boys on their improvised tram

Picture by Jane Flower

Water, Water...

There were two deputies whose duty it was to inspect the shaft daily. They were lowered down in the doorless cage at slow speed and each had a high candle-power lamp to search for any problems that might be revealed in the shaft linings. I had become friendly with another Bevin Boy who was a keen cyclist. For some reason he was known as Luke – I never really found out why. There was something of the explorer in him. At weekends he would be off on his bike putting in unbelievable distances and finding out about the countryside in a way that was impossible in any other way but on a bike.

His thirst for geographical knowledge was not confined to the surface. We had noticed that the deputies and the manager had a habit of appearing as if from nowhere in our district, the Old Three South. They had not come from the main North via the normal haulage roads. Therefore we argued there must be a way between the two districts not known to the main work-force. We would find it. At the end of the shift we tarried as everybody else made their way out and then we set off in the direction of the secret route used by the officials.

We were eagerly looking forward to seeing the expressions of amazement that would show on the faces of our colleagues when they got to the pit bottom and we were there before them. It did not work out quite like that.

Not very long after the start of our foray into the unknown we arrived at a sort of junction. As you might expect we took the wrong branch. Perhaps the lack of rails and the presence of undisturbed dust should have told us that this was an unused heading. Eventually we came to an obstruction – props nailed together in the form of a cross, a sure indication that no one must pass that point. We turned round and retraced our steps back to the junction and then took the other way. Again we came to a dead end. We soon realised that we were lost. Our joint spirit of adventure had led us astray. We were beginning to get alarmed, although neither would admit it to the other. We knew that we would be missed and that perhaps we might be found but no one would know where to start looking for us. We pressed on and you can imagine our relief when we stumbled into the main haulage way, but nowhere near the pit bottom.

We had to start the long trudge to the pit bottom. It was when we were almost there that we saw two lights coming in our direction. The lamps were carried by two very irate deputies who had discovered that we were missing. They had been obliged to come back from the surface to search for us when they discovered we were not accounted for.

Because of our quest for adventure Luke and I had kept them at work longer than usual. They expressed their annoyance, but politely informed us that theirs was as nothing to that of the winding engine man who had been pulled away from his favourite dinner to let them down the pit to search for us. But it was a macho thrill to go up the shaft in the cage without its man riding gates. We took the highly dangerous opportunity to lean out of the cage and look upwards to see what the top of the shaft looked like from a long way down. All we could see was a tiny intricate pattern of girders high above in the blackness.

At least we now knew what it was like to look up the shaft and find out what it looked like from the bottom. As it happened the two deputies were mildly amused at our curiosity and bore us no ill will for our adventure. Eventually the manager rapped our knuckles and told us not to do it again. So that was how we got a ride in a cage without doors.

As we came up it was interesting to see the traces of water occasionally trickling down the walls of the shaft. Ours was not a wet pit even though not particularly deep. What water there was drained into the sump at the bottom of the shaft and was then pumped to the surface. On the main haulage way, about half a mile in, there was a depression colloquially called the swilly. Here there would occasionally be water but a small pump dealt with that.

I never thought a great deal about water. At one time or another I had considered most of the catastrophes which could happen, but I had never really given much attention to fear of water. The fear must have been lurking there in my subconscious. My father told me one evening – I never saw him until the evening – that I had woken him the previous night by yelling in my sleep, 'Look out, there is water in the airway!' I had no recollection of any nightmare, but it is well we cannot remember all our dreams.

1947 had started with a harsh and long winter, one of the worst during the twentieth century, but the ensuing summer, my third as a miner, became a long hot summer, one of those we are told occurs before a war breaks out. But as it was only two years since the war had finished, nobody could be bothered thinking of the possibility of another war, not just yet.

Reports began to appear in the newspapers of sporadic outbreaks of poliomyelitis – infantile paralysis as it was called in those days. Insidiously it was soon to reach epidemic proportions, but, of course, this was something that only happened to others.

It was always depressing having to spend a third of the day in darkness, more so when the weather was wonderful on the surface. It was now that I was sent to tram for Wilf Kellett. He was an easy going sort of chap who did not complain much. It could be for that reason that he had the lowest gate on the face. And now water was beginning to appear. The face was on a slight gradient. This meant that every morning there would be about six inches of water at the end of the face. This does not sound much but it had to be shifted before work could start in any sort of comfort. There were a couple of tubs provided for this contingency. They were just the same as the standard wooden tubs, but they had been caulked to render them waterproof. The top was half decked over with a sliding door which could be slid open to fill them with water, and then closed to prevent the contents from slopping out on the rough ride to the pit bottom.

At first it meant filling these tubs with the shovels, not ideal tools for moving water, but as the water became more insistent, Wilf brought a *piggin* in one day. This was the mid-Pennine word for a lading can. With this it was much easier to fill the water tubs before the real work could begin. The water always looked black and evil in the dark with its layer of dust scumming the surface.

When we managed to get rid of the water, the floor was still wet and greasy, and extremely unpleasant to lie on. So Wilf got himself what the miners called a buffet.

This was a square of wooden boards about eighteen inches square. The boards were held together by two crosspieces. The result was a sort of platform which you could rest on about three inches above the surface of the wet floor, and work away at the coal-face.

It was not a happy experience. Not only was it wet and cold but the mixture of dust and water tended to soak into your clothes then set like cement when it eventually began to dry. I never found out how long Wilf had to work in these conditions but I always thanked my lucky stars that presumably some day there would be an end to it for me, even though at that time I could see no prospect of the release from my life as a miner. And what would I do when that happy release came?

How Much Longer?

The war had been over for two years but there was no sign yet of our release from our enforced labour. We looked with envy on slightly older friends who were no longer in the forces, spending their gratuities and strutting about in their ill fitting demob suits. Would there be any reward for us? All we wanted was to get out and to restart our lives. The only consolation was that we were now on top of the work we had to do, more able to cope with what was necessary. But no matter what time it was that you went to bed at night, it was always a spine-chilling shock when the alarm clock announced the start of another day, invariably only moments after your head had hit the pillow the previous night. I don't think I knew what sleepless nights were in those days.

I would roll out of bed and try to eat a breakfast of toast and Marmite washed down with vintage cocoa, while I huddled over a small portable gas fire, my knees on either side, funnelling the feeble warmth up my ex-ARP (Air Raid Precautions) greatcoat. These were the same as army greatcoats but dyed a different colour and bought cheaply at war surplus stores. I would shamble off into the morning darkness and knock on Alf's front door. With a barely noticeable gruff greeting we would then begin the mile and a half walk to the bus stop, without a word between us.

We walked past the shop of the Misses Peacock – they sold sweets, tobacco and newspapers. There would be a glimmer of light in the back of the shop in the middle of the night as the two industrious sisters prepared to open their lock-up shop for the day. They were what in those days were described as maiden ladies. No one had any reason to doubt this as being a true and accurate description. They were rumoured to be incredibly wealthy and again nobody doubted but what this would be true. During times of shortage and rationing they were noted for having 'just sold the last packet' of either sweets or cigarettes. It was accepted that they had an arrangement with their providers to supply them with last packets only. It was but a favoured few who managed to get any contraband, never mind legal supplies out of the Misses Peacock.

At the bus stop there would be about half a dozen other regulars but not all miners. Some were bound for an early start in various textile mills, but they all stood with heads hunched down into shoulders, huddled round the lamp-post which served as a bus stop. They radiated that negative feeling of well-being and enthusiasm notably lacking in all of those who start work in the middle of the night. The odd one who was in favour with the Misses Peacock would have half a tab smouldering at his lips, but in the dim light of the immediate post-war years they exhibited all the cheerfulness of a German expressionist woodcut.

The bus would come chugging up the hill out of the gloom of the town centre half-laden with half-frozen early morning workers who scarcely exchanged a word apart from complaining if they thought the bus conductor had given them wrong change.

You would then snuggle into your seat, and after about fifteen minutes you became quite warm and cosy and drifted off into a velvety sleep when the bus would jerk to a stop and the conductor or more usually the conductress would vigorously shake your shoulder if there was any danger of being taken past your stop.

Then, still with heads down, we would shamble along avoiding the puddles or patches of ice along the pit lane to the lamp room. Then up the stairs to the pit-head or bank as it is often called, where the banksman would occasionally make a show of frisking us to make sure we were not taking any 'contraband' – cigarettes, matches, lighters, and so on – below. Standing in a submissive orderly queue we were beginning to wake up and starting to come back to life as we were lowered down below, four men at a time to the bottom of the shaft. While it was a cold pit it was always warmer down below than it was on top in winter, so it was some sort of relief to get down below. On this particular morning the deputy who was wearing the under manager hat told me that today he wanted me to go by-working with Eddie James and to help him in driving a new heading in the Old Three South. This was a subsidiary district with a face at right angles to the main North face. There was a junction on the main haulage plane where another road gave access to the Old Three South. This is the point where Herbert worked. No one seemed to know if he had a surname, but his job was both responsible and skilled. He had to act as signal man and stop the runs of tubs in exactly the right place in order to exchange the haulage ropes to serve the appropriate arm of the junction. These couplings were some distance along the rope from the train of tubs and were for joining one rope to another.

If the signal man did not get his signal right it meant that one rope or the other would have to be manhandled into position in order to join up with its new connection – very strenuous work indeed.

The very nature of his work meant that Herbert spent a lot of time by himself with only the hiss of the running rope to keep him company. But, on the other hand, his lonely junction tended to become a place where people on the move would stop to *cal* or chat – have *a bit crack* as they would say farther north. The geographical location of Herbert's junction was somewhere below the old LNW railway line from Leeds to Manchester and Herbert claimed he could hear the trains as they rumbled above his lonely junction. The line would be about 300 feet above and I always found it difficult to believe that the trains could be heard. I never had the chance to sit with him and listen but he was adamant. We challenged him to identify the type of locomotive; was it a Black Five or a Horwich 'Crab'? Herbert did not know. 'It was just a train, see?' Such little arguments brightened the darkness and gloom for a while.

As I made my way to the new heading I had no idea of the excitement which lay ahead. The heading had only been driven about twelve feet and our job this particular morning was to drill a shot hole, get the deputy to come and fire a shot, and then we would have to tram the fallen rock away. We did not have shot-firers as such and this responsible work was done by a deputy. Eddie decided where the shot hole should be drilled and assembled the drill. We had no powered machinery so this was a hand drill. It was a simple frame which was wedged between roof and floor. A threaded casting rested in one of a series of holes and enabled the hand-turned drill to react against it and thus penetrate the rock. It was hard monotonous work even when there were two of you doing the drilling.

When we had drilled the hole to the required depth, we waited for the deputy to come and plant the explosive to blast the rock. The deputy came, asked how we were and had a bit of a chat. Then he took his explosive, attached the fuse and wires and tamped it into the shot hole which we had just bored. He then told us to get back to a refuge hole some distance away. He reeled out his cable to the refuge hole and connected it to his shot-firing battery unit and asked if we were all ready for the bang. We told him we were so he flicked the switch.

Nothing happened.

We looked at one another. The deputy said he would try again. He did; still nothing happened. He tested his battery and made several attempts, but the more he tried, the explosive seemed to be more determined not to oblige. At last in a fit of annoyance he told us we would have to drill another hole. He would go to disconnect the wires and try to make sure everything was safe. Both Eddie and I wished him luck and expressed the thought that it was better he went to do this as he was more highly qualified for such hazardous missions than we were. He then went up to the rock face and detached the wires. Next he drew a cross on the roof above our bore hole with the piece of chalk which was part of a deputy's standard equipment. Then he measured one foot to the right of this and drew another cross. One foot was the minimum distance apparently for a second charge to be placed. He told us to bore another hole below his second cross and he would return to place another charge.

Grudgingly we drilled another hole in the rock, which was obviously harder than coal. Just as we had achieved the required depth, the deputy reappeared and said he would have another go.

Eddie and I retired again to the refuge hole which wasn't all that far from the site as the deputy followed his previous procedure. We huddled together in the refuge hole as the deputy connected up and asked us if we were ready. We nodded our assent and he threw the switch.

At the callow age of twenty I had not given much thought as to what the end of the world would be like. I suddenly realised that I was now probably in the middle of it, experiencing the awful last trump of doom. There seemed to be a brilliant flash of whiteness which just as quickly went a dirty greyish black. My ears were whistling and I was choked with dust. Even though our lamps were still alight we could see nothing in the thick blanket of dust. I did not know which way to go and I don't think either Eddie or the deputy had much idea. We were down on our knees and instinctively crawling along the rails, where they were not covered with shattered rock. Fortunately we went in the right direction. We found our way into the main crossgate where the air was moving and began to work out what had happened. The dust settled and we went back to see the damage. The deputy examined his markings on the roof and decided we had drilled the second hole in the correct place.

What he thought must have happened was that our second drilling had been deflected towards the position of the first shot of explosive, the one still in place – there was no way of getting it out once it was tamped into position. When the second shot was fired it had been near enough to the first to cause them both to explode in sympathy.

My ears were still singing and it was some time before I could hear conversation without the speaker having to shout.

This was just a mishap and not worthy of an enquiry or any trouble like that. Eddie and I got on with the job of clearing up and I was glad when it was the end of the shift. I did not want to have many experiences like this, one which did not actually encourage me to embrace mining as a permanent profession. Not a long time previously I had made enquiries with the same deputy about training for the mine rescue service, but this incident nipped the idea in the bud. On the way home Alf remarked that I was a bit quieter than usual, but we didn't talk much about things like that. The next day I was back to tramming for colliers. It was good to be away from the vicinity of explosives. But I was more eager than ever to see the light of day all day long and every day, but as yet there was no break in the dark clouds and little hope for a future early release. But my escape was to come sooner than I hoped in a totally different way to any I had expected.

The End is Nigh...

It was the beginning of August in 1947. Already it was showing promise of being a warm summer; the long lasting snows of the recent long winter were forgotten. Only the thoughts of eight hours down the pit spoilt the beauty of those early mornings as the sun began to climb in the skies already blue. But while most of our miners acknowledged each other with some sort of greeting ranging from 'Ow, Harry' to a polite 'Good morning', or even 'Good day' few really took much notice of the splendour of the morning which not long ago had been the middle of the night.

The greeting 'Ow, Harry' was a colloquialism. It could carry a wealth of meaning in its subtle expression. The reply invariably would be 'Ow, Bert'. And this response would echo the content of the original greeting, whether cheerful or sad, joyful or just non-committal. These were men of few words who would speak when they had something to say. It was futile to attempt to join in their system of communication, at least until you were fully accepted.

The older men would be pleased to receive their full title from us lads. 'Good morning, Mr Wakelin. How is your allotment doing?' or something similar would always go down well. This was a Wednesday and my hopes were that the weather would not break during the next three or four weeks, because in two weeks' time it would be the annual holiday week when the pit closed down – Bowling Tide week as it was known in this part of the industrial West Riding. It was known also for being a week of traditional wet weather, whether spent at Blackpool, Morecambe, Scarborough or Whitby. It would even rain on the more adventurous who went further afield to exotic Cleethorpes or Skegness. I have never really discovered the origin of Bowling Tide. It must have something to do with the archaic word for time, as in the phrase 'Time and Tide wait for no man!' The tide at the seaside never came in as far as Bowling.

Bowling Tide week was the week when the fair came to a bit of spare ground in the district of Bowling. As children we would look forward to the 'Tide' coming. It was nowhere near the size of the fair at Hull or the Tyneside Hoppings. But it was magic with its gleaming, shining showmen's traction engines, the bags of brandysnap, each with a picture of one of these magnificent engines printed on it and the hunger-making smell of frying chips.

The terrifying steam launches Shamrock and Columbine, giant swings which swung to dizzying heights from which there was no escape once they had started, encouraged you to forget all about having any more chips and brandysnap. Another favourite was the Caterpillar, a rare device with a vast array of wheels and a hood which, once it had been set in motion, hid the riders from view. I suppose it did look a bit like a circular caterpillar, but it was quite a time before I realised the significance of the hood and the screams which invariably issued from beneath its capacious confines.

It is now a long time since a factory was built on the site of the Bowling Tide, but that particular week is still known as Bowling Tide week, no matter where the showmen pitch their fair; and it still rains during this summer holiday week.

But now I was above all this. My idea of a holiday was to go exploring the Dales with a group of friends or even the Lake District when we could sort out the transport there. It was not to be very long before I would be free from the pit for a week. The day started off as normal but by the time it came for us to have our break the work was beginning to feel much harder. I just could not face eating my sandwiches. Somebody asked me if I was feeling all right. I said that I was, but I did not really mean it. I managed to finish the shift with a grim determination which surprised me, as under normal circumstances anything to get a doctor's note was welcomed. But I carried on. On top at the end of the shift I told Alf that I would miss my canteen meal and that I would catch an earlier bus home. He said I looked a bit off it, even under the grime and dirt of the pit.

When I got home I staggered upstairs and flaked out on my

bed, no attempt to have a bath or eat anything. I was beginning to feel a blinding headache like a tight band of hot iron round my head and getting tighter. My parents came home from a day out as part of their stay-at-home holiday and called in the doctor. He asked me if I could lift my head from the pillow. I couldn't.

He frowned and shook his head. 'You will have to go to hospital,' was his terse comment. 'They will take a sample of spinal fluid to determine what this is.'

Up to this point I had always had robust health. My own thoughts were that I had picked up a bad cold or something and that in two or three days I would be back to normal, but the headache was frightening. At the isolation hospital they took a sample of spinal fluid and from that moment the headache began to subside. I was very weak, but that was okay. Any time now they would tell me that there had been a mis-diagnosis – all that was wrong was that I had a touch of 'flu and in a few days I would be fit again and able to go on my holiday. But they never did come to tell me that there had been a mistake.

That year there was an epidemic of poliomyelitis, infantile paralysis as it was known fifty years ago, although in 1947 it was seen to be a misnomer. At that time I did not realise how ill I was, or what was happening to me. Relatives and friends were allowed to visit but they could only stand outside and look through the windows. I was on some sort of danger list. I was given a code number with my condition which was both published in the evening paper and posted in a window of the Town Hall – they didn't have civic centres in those days. After three weeks of utter helplessness in the fever hospital, I was transferred to a general hospital, where I was to spend several long weary months facing up to an unknown future. In a time of uncertainty, there was but one certainty, I would no longer have to go down the pit.

It was just before Christmas that I was eventually allowed home. It was another five months before I began working again. But not down the pit. I had found lasting friends; my life in the mining industry was rapidly becoming something of a bad dream.

I may have thought of going in for mining properly at one time by taking exams and so on – although even now I couldn't pass an exam to save my life. It was only after my absence from the pit that I realised how horrible it had all been. The men at the pit where I worked had made a generous collection for me when they had heard of my plight. Most of them would have to go working there forever, but I was now free.

During the sixties and seventies when the pits were being closed I felt a conflicting sense of both relief and regret at each announcement of a closure. I had known what it was to get coal, I had known what it was to sweat like a pig, although I have never seen pigs sweat like we did. I knew what it was to come home caked up with the mixture of water, sweat and pit-dust mud that set like concrete in your working clothes. I wondered why sons wanted to follow their fathers in this trade, and even why fathers would want to encourage sons to follow them.

But then I had not been born to it. The sooner every pit was closed the sooner life would be safer for many thousands of men as far as I was concerned. No doubt it was character forming whatever that may mean, and I certainly met a great number of unforgettable characters. It was without any doubt a man's job.

The great Miner's Strike was a reminder of how much the mining force wanted to continue a way of life in which I, for a short time, reluctantly had to take part.

Epilogue

A year or two after I found my feet again I was earning a living taking photographs for local newspapers. One day I was asked to go and look at a report of a fire at a local colliery.

Imagine my delight when I found that it was in the pit where I once worked. The reports were exaggerated. Rubbish had caught fire and eager witnesses exaggerated the inferno. I arrived and dutifully reported to the weighman's office to ask about the disaster. I was told politely that there was nothing to see. As I turned to leave, my old manager appeared on the scene and seeing my camera demanded to know what I was doing on his premises. He told me that I should be minding my own business and that he did not believe in newspapers and I had better leave at once. This was a marked change in attitude from the times in the past when he had eagerly welcomed national press representatives to report record production from his pit.

I was complying with his request when suddenly he called me back. 'Don't I know thee?' looking me straight in the eyes. I confirmed that he ought to do as I had worked for him as one of his Bevin Boys. His face lit up. 'We've come a long way since you left, lad. We've now got conveyors and all sorts of improvements below. If you've got time I'll tak' thee down now and show thee round, tha'll be impressed.' I had to decline; anyway, I wasn't dressed for such a visit, although that did not seem to bother him. He seemed disappointed, this man who had constantly reminded we Bevin Boys what a useless lot we were. 'Have you got a few minutes then, lad? Ah'd like thee to meet somebody.' I agreed because he seemed so pleased to see me. He took me to the canteen which had now been extended and where there was a room for the deputies. There were about six of them beginning a meal at the end of their shift. The canteen dinner was still just as welcome after a day's work.

The manager showed me in. The men began to preen

themselves as if they all thought they were going to have their photographs taken for some reason.

'You lot, look at this young man! He was one of my Bevin Boys an' if you lot worked half as hard as he and his mates did this pit 'ud happen get somewhere!'

I gave a sickly sort of smile as the extent of my embarrassment began to sink in. I attempted an apology to the overseers and tried to suggest that memory and the fullness of time had enhanced our qualities in the manager's mind, but he would have none of it.

This incident reminded me of the time when I was at my worst in hospital and some experts were doubting that I would ever lead a useful life again. It may well be that my old colliery manager would have agreed with their diagnosis spending the rest of my working life as I did in newspapers.

A scene-setting artist's impression capturing the joy of the Bevin Boy's existence
By Jane Flower

Printed in the United States
47743LVS00001BA/123